Finding Jesus In Sobriety

FINDING JESUS IN SOBRIETY

A Millennial Translation of the Gospel of Mark

John C. Mellon

Markos Books
EVANSTON, ILLINOIS

Printed in the United States of America

Published by Markos Books
Box 6131, Evanston, IL 60204

Cover by Metzler Design, Downers Grove, IL

Alcoholics Anonymous has neither reviewed nor approved the contents of this book, and references to A.A. should not be taken to mean that Alcoholics Anonymous agrees with the ideas expressed herein.

Publisher's Cataloging-in-Publication Data
(Provided by Quality Books, Inc.)

Bible. N.T. Mark. English. Mellon. 1999
Finding Jesus in sobriety : a millennial translation of the Gospel of Mark / John C. Mellon.—1st ed.
p. cm.
Includes bibliographical references.
Library of Congress Catalog Card Number: 98-91775
ISBN: 0-9666431-2-7 (alk. paper)

1. Bible. N.T. Mark—Commentaries. 2. Jesus Christ. 3. Twelve-step programs—Religious aspects—Christianity. 4. Drinking in the Bible. I. Mellon, John C. II. Title.

BS2583.M433 1999 226.3'05209
QBI98-1172

For
All Cupmasters

Contents

Preface

While I hope that New Testament scholars and many other people will read this book, I extend a particular invitation to recovering alcoholics.

If you find yourself attracted to Jesus but feel that something is lacking, perhaps even inauthentic in what you hear about him in churches or read in the other gospels, this translation of Mark is for you.

For the Jesus in this book is not the Jesus of Christianity. This Jesus is an alcoholic who, happily for all, receives the gift of sobriety. But not the first time around. First he has to relapse, suffer more, and finally admit his powerlessness over self as well as alcohol. This is his story as told in the Gospel of Mark.

For nineteen hundred years this story has remained hidden in Mark's original Greek, invisible to Christian eyes and absent from vernacular translations. Two factors have brought it to light now. First, the spirituality and lore of Alcoholics Anonymous provide a context, previously unavailable, for interpreting Jesus' career in terms of addiction. Second, a study of the ambiguities (double meanings) in the Greek text reveals two distinct portrayals of Jesus, one of them that of a former wine addict.

I invite you to meet that man in this book, a man afflicted by anger and combativeness in his effort to advance the movement he has founded; a relapser cut off for a time from his program and his Higher Power; a visionary who, in a burst of apocalyptic insight, sees the role of alcohol in God's plan for human redemption; and finally a surrendered person who invites the many to drink their way to sobriety, then shows them how to die to self and so arise to eternal life.

Although Jesus had a destiny far more notable than ours, I believe he shared with addicts everywhere both the pangs of the alcoholic illness and the glories of recovery.

Ancient Recovery Oracle

Awake, o people, awake!
You who have drunk from God's hand
  the cup of anger,
Who have drained to the bottom
  the chalice of drunkenness.
These two afflictions have befallen you,
  who can relieve your pain?

Thus replies Yahweh, God of Power,
  who defends the cause of his people:
"Listen to this, all you addicted to drink,
  and you who are drunk but not with wine.
"Look, I take from your hand
  the chalice of drunkenness,
"And the cup of anger you shall
  not have to drink again,
"For I will put it in the hands of those
  who seek to dominate and control."

So awake, I say, awake and claim your power!
  Arise, captives, and throw off your bondage!
For you were not addicted for a price,
  and are freed not by money but by gift.

From Second Isaiah 51.17-52.3, ca 550 B.C.E. This oracle on addiction and recovery may have prompted Jesus to interpret the Suffering Servant Poem (Is 52.13-53.12) in a similar light.

Introduction

For almost twenty years, the period of my recovery from active alcoholism, I have pondered and prayed over the textual enigmas in the Gospel of Mark. Recently I published my conclusions in an academic book, *Mark as Recovery Story* (University of Illinois Press, 1995). In it I argue that the Greek text of Mark contains not one gospel but two, whose differences come to light when we view that text through different interpretive frameworks. I call these frameworks Christian Mark and Sobriety Mark. As evidence of the latter, my book presents many new and surprising readings of Mark's Greek, translations based upon alternative understandings of the gospel's ambiguities and secrecy emblems.

These newly discovered readings indicate that Mark wrote for a dual audience, twin communities of readers on the scene in Palestine around 68 A.D. One of these communities, the readers of Christian Mark, consisted of Messianic Jesus people hoping to survive Roman reprisals after the ongoing war by leaving Judaism and embracing Christianity. The other community, the readers of Sobriety Mark, was a regional fellowship of former wine addicts whose ideas about powerlessness and spiritual empowerment foreshadowed those of Alcoholics Anonymous today. While both communities considered Jesus their founder, they held quite different views of his spirituality and martyrdom.

This theory of the Gospel of Mark stands or falls on the acceptability of the alternative translations ascribed to Sobriety Mark. These are difficult to evaluate, however, because the only available framework for assessing them is that of Christian Mark, wherein they seem out of place. What is needed, and what I have undertaken here, is a full translation of Sobriety Mark providing an appropriate context of interpretation for readers wishing to gauge the validity of its individual parts.

By full translation I mean more than merely English words in place of Greek words. I mean a version whose word meanings are glossed, whose reference relationships are stated, whose ellipses (textual omissions) are restored, whose symbolism is identified, and whose background assumptions are spelled out; in short, a version reflecting the interpretive mindset of the community for whom Sobriety Mark was intended. Such fullness is unnecessary in translations of Christian Mark because readers already know its religious meaning. It *is* necessary, however, for persons wishing to examine the Gospel of Mark from perspectives other than that of Christianity.

Background

Again, the argument of Sobriety Mark is that Jesus' original following, as well as Mark's "insider" audience almost forty years later, consisted of recovering alcoholics. This idea flies in the face of tradition and raises a host of questions, some of which should be answered now.

Alcoholism in Antiquity Chronic drunkenness—"alcoholism" in modern terminology—is well documented among ancient beer and wine drinkers, and recovery fellowships unknown to history could have existed in the first century just as today. Jesus' homeland was known for its wines, and archaeologists in Nazareth have recently excavated the limestone basin used as the town winepress. Galileans predisposed to alcohol addiction could hardly have escaped contracting the illness.

Jesus' Story Mark's gospel contains the first narrative of Jesus' career from his Jordan baptism to the crisis in Jerusalem. While collections of Jesus' sayings may have predated Mark, the idea that Mark's narrative reflects settled tradition, written or oral, cannot be verified. Paul's letters, for example, contain no information about Jesus' life other than his death. Until Mark there *is* no Jesus story. Hence Mark was free to employ ambiguous representation and allegory (rhetorical devices well known in ancient writing) to chronicle for his Christian audience the mighty works of a heroic son of God ending with a crucifixion and an empty tomb, and for his sobriety fellowship the narrative of a drunken and messianic son of man ending with a spiritual surrender and recovery. It was, I think, the latter story that Mark believed actual. The former he recognized as the product of the

Christianizing of Jesus' story.

Who Wrote Mark? Together with many scholars, I believe that the writer surnamed/nicknamed Mark was the John Mark of the Book of Acts. As a young man he first met Jesus during the Jerusalem Passover, thereafter served briefly as a co-worker with the apostle Paul, and years later, in his late fifties, wrote his gospel. In it Mark portrays himself as the young follower of Jesus who runs away naked when Jesus is arrested (Mark 14.51-52), and in an earlier version of his book (The Secret Gospel of Mark[1]) depicts his entrance into Jesus' recovery fellowship.

Mark's Nicknames Two nicknames of the gospel writer have survived, Mark and stump-fingered. Both point to recovery from alcohol addiction. The Greco-Roman form of Mark was Marcus, a common name in the Gentile world. To multilingual Palestinian Jews, Marcus sounded like the Hebrew/Aramaic phrase *mar* (lord or master) *kôs* (cup). Markôs, or cupmaster, among other possible meanings, designates a victor over the ravages of wine addiction. As such, Marcus/Markôs would have served as a coterie name not just for John Mark but for all members of his sobriety fellowship. Similarly, the name "stump-fingered," which the Anti-Marcionite Prologue applies to Mark,[2] would have referred to one who cannot grasp a drinking vessel, who cannot take up the winecup, in other words, figuratively, a person who cannot drink normally so no longer drinks at all. In short, stump-fingered was ancient slang for former drunkard. Just as today's addicts say, "I'm a recovering alcoholic, sober today," Mark and his cohorts would have said, "I'm a markôs, stump-fingered today." Throughout this book I refer to members of Jesus' recovery community as Markôs people or Cupmasters.

Why Mark Wrote Mark's visit to Peter in Rome to obtain details of Jesus' Galilean ministry some years before he wrote suggests a longstanding plan to compose a narrative of Jesus' career.[3] What triggered Mark's project was the Roman-Jewish War. I believe he expected the worst as he surveyed the situation in Judea during the lull in the fighting in 68 A.D., not just destruction of the Temple but the scattering of the populace and the end of Judean Judaism and the haven it had provided his recovery movement.[4] (The Cupmasters presumably met in synagogues just as A.A. meets in church basements today.) Mark felt that it was his final opportunity to write the story of Jesus and the Markôs fellowship, but how best to guarantee the preservation of his book for future generations?

Apparently Mark heard about a survival strategy planned by Messianic Jews who, in order to stave off Roman savagery, were prepared to renounce their Judaism, call themselves Christian, appoint bishops and deacons like the Gentile churches, and petition for peace with the Romans. Mark recognized that to authenticate their claim to be Christians, these groups would need a work of scripture recounting the saga of Jesus Messiah (Christ). Here was his chance: he would write the gospel required by his Messianic friends—Christian Mark—but into it he would secretly weave the true story of the alcoholic Jesus known to the Markôs people—Sobriety Mark—confident that the Christian community would discern only the religious image of Jesus.

Mark's plan was clearly successful. History records no cases of Roman persecution of Jewish Christians in Palestine after 70 A.D. The hostile synagogue prayers that postwar Jews directed against Jewish Christians suggest that the latter had indeed grown in numbers.[5] Mark's book enjoyed sufficient favor among Jewish and Gentile Christians to be incorporated into Matthew's and Luke's gospels without significant alteration of its narrative content. The Markôs movement, overrun by a postwar tide of abstinent ascetics who were not inebriates,[6] probably went deeper underground and ultimately disappeared in the crosscurrents of second-century gnosticism. Not until the advent of Alcoholics Anonymous would a successor community appear capable of discerning Sobriety Mark in the gospel's Greek text.

Jesus As Alcoholic Jesus' alcoholism underlies all the familiar events of the Markan narrative. The following overview suggests how those events are portrayed in Sobriety Mark:

a) Pursuit of relief from his wine addiction explains Jesus' otherwise unexplained journey to the Jordan River, where his story begins.

b) His baptism there recalls his turn from wine to water; the wilderness experience reflects detoxification; demon possession figures the wine devil in drinkers; and the "cup of water to drink" (9.41) is the Markôs entrance rite.

c) His decision to go to Jerusalem flows from his alcoholic compulsion to play God; the Aramaic "donkey/wine" pun backgrounding the Jerusalem entrance story points to his return to active drinking; his violent attempt to seize the wine vessels of Temple worshippers (11.16, as translated here) results from intoxication combined with mental drunkenness.

d) The apocalyptic discourse (chap. 13) recalls his hangover revelation about the turning point and onset of recovery.

e) The man carrying water rather than wine for Passover (14.13) signifies that the Jerusalem seder was a Markôs meeting. At the supper, Jesus identifies wine as the cause of his troubles and announces his decision to drink no more.

f) His prayer in Gethsemane, a placename possibly meaning Sign of the Winepress,[7] begins with a humble request for help to get through the moment at hand, and concludes with his admission of powerlessness, request for removal of his cup addiction, and renunciation of self-will, actions today's alcoholics will recognize as a Step Three surrender.

Bits of extra-Markan evidence exist as well.[8] The Sayings Gospel Q, reflected in Matthew 11.18-19 and Luke 7.33-35, obliquely refers to Jesus' reputation as an unbridled drunkard. The Gospel of Thomas (logion 28) preserves Jesus' pronouncement on addiction and recovery: "While men drink they remain drunk; when they abjure their wine their thinking is changed." The infamous anti-Christian Celsus describes Jesus at the crucifixion "rushing with his mouth open to drink," a slander recalling Jesus' reputation as an inebriate. Pagan images depicting Christ as donkey-headed reflect a misunderstanding of the northern Aramaic donkey/wine pun suggesting that Jesus and the Markôs people were referred to as wineheads. The story of the supposed wine miracle at Cana in the Gospel of John, minus the spurious phrase "made wine" (2.9), actually depicts Jesus' substitution of water for wine, the entrance rite into recovery. Many of the early Christian communities who drank their communion in water not wine, a practice invariably said to reflect asceticism, were actually Markôs groups. The saying in Hebrews 10.29 promising punishment for anyone who "deems unclean the blood of the covenant by which he was sanctified," that is, who refuses to drink the eucharistic wine, represents a Christian anathema against the abstinent Markôs people. And the Pentecost story in Acts 2.12-16 inadvertently preserves the apostles' reputations as drunkards.

Addiction and Recovery

Persons with no experience of addiction and recovery cannot comprehend Sobriety Mark without guidance. I find that former addicts generally need help as well. Everyone's understandings of Jesus reflect belief systems so culturally ingrained that invitations to think about Jesus' career in non-Christian ways often produce confusion and rejection, especially when the alternative paradigm is as poorly understood as alcoholism. The following information should help all persons read Sobriety Mark successfully.

Alcoholism Most sober alcoholics understand alcoholism as a spiritual illness. Its symptoms are a seemingly unbreakable dependence on alcohol coupled with fear, anger, dishonesty, denial, and attempts to be God for oneself. It has nothing to do with how much one drinks or how often, or what kind of drunken behaviors one exhibits. Successful treatment begins with self diagnosis, and the diagnostic opinions of others, professional or lay, are largely irrelevant. Merely quitting drinking does not cure or even arrest alcoholism, it only enables the sufferer to begin the program of spiritual living necessary for recovery.

Drunkenness Recovering persons identify two kinds of drunkenness, physical and mental. Everyone is familiar with the physical kind. Mental drunkenness manifests itself in grandiosity, self will, judgmentalness, the compulsion to control others, anger, and self-pity. Mental drunkenness occurs apart from physical, but is most harmful when catalyzed by drink. The term mental drunkenness is metaphorical but the condition it names is real. In Jesus' case, it is physical drunkenness that brings him to the Jordan for relief from wine addiction, then mental drunkenness that compels him, after his troubles in Galilee, to go to Jerusalem where he drinks again and engages in the violence and rhetorical combat that bring him to crisis.

Turning Point Turning points are moments of grace when drinkers "hit bottom," admit powerlessness, and experience the desire to quit drinking. Jesus' first turning point is his baptism. His second immediately follows his apocalypse (revelation) in Jerusalem, when he realizes what he must do at the supper and in Gethsemane.

Changed Thinking Recovery requires a change from drunk thinking to sober thinking. Alcoholics speak about the necessity of "changing everything about yourself." Mark's term for this process is *metanoia*, a Greek verb ordinarily translated "repent" whose root meaning is: change your mind, understand differently. It is the word Mark uses for John the Baptist's call to repentance (1.4) and Jesus' invitation to recovery (1.15).

Higher Power Lack of power is the addict's dilemma. Recovering persons have learned that admitting powerlessness brings help from a power greater than self, a Higher Power most alcoholics refer to as "God as we understand Him." An important question in Mark's gospel is power (*dunamis*) and who has it, God or man. Jesus' surrender in Gethsemane is to a God whom he calls *Abba* (father) and understands as the source of all *dunamis*.

Water From time immemorial, water has been a counter-symbol to wine and other alcoholic drink. This is why Jordan water, the cup of water, and the mysterious water carrier are salient textual emblems in Sobriety Mark.

Recovery Recovery involves asking for help, attending meetings, efforts to change, and placing one's life in the care of God. Fittingly, the name of the Markans' recovery program was the Rule of God. Elements of Sobriety Mark indicating recovery are Jesus' calls for a changing of mind, joining in a following, maintaining anonymity, and meeting apart from the multitude, together with parables on the importance the Rule of God.

Two-stages Recovery typically occurs in two stages separated by an interval, powerlessness over alcohol followed by powerlessness over self. For Jesus, stage one occurs at the Jordan, stage two in Jerusalem. The stage-one/stage-two imagery in Mark points to this phenomenon as an organizing principle of the gospel.

Honeymoon Alcoholics use the term honeymoon to refer to the euphoric period after release from alcohol but before the recognition of one's mental drunkenness. Premature and self-willed attempts to carry the message to others ("two-stepping" in A.A. parlance) often end the honeymoon and lead to anger, messianism, and a relapse into drinking. This is Jesus' fate as his efforts in Galilee begin to fail and he embarks on his fateful mission to Jerusalem.

Twelve Steps The Twelve Steps of Alcoholics Anonymous set forth a sequence of actions that lead to spiritual awakening and useful living. In Mark 3.14-15 the word "Twelve" occurs as a proper adjective without a following noun in connection with the ambiguous Greek verb *poieō,* which can mean either "appoint" or "formulate" depending upon its noun. In Christian Mark Twelve refers to the twelve disciples Jesus appointed, while in Sobriety Mark it refers to twelve precepts of recovery Jesus formulated, similar in purpose to A.A.'s Twelve Steps.

Meeting and Eating Sober people attend meetings (A.A., Al-Anon, etc.) where they hear one another's stories and discuss the Twelve Steps. Markan references to drawing apart from the crowds and gatherings with the Twelve are code terms for meetings of the Markôs fellowship. Meetings in Mark are represented as table fellowship or outdoor gatherings wherein bread is a metaphor for the words of recovery distributed by those who tell their stories and multiplied in the followup comments of listeners. Mark's accounts of feeding the multitudes, multiplying bread, calming stormy seas, and walking on water are narrative versions of parables that Jesus told about meetings and the serenity they produce.

Spiritual Awakening A.A.'s twelfth step promises an awakening to Spirit, a resurrection to new life after the spiritual death of addiction. Jesus' references to being lifted up and empowered and to bearing witness for the benefit of others (13.26, 14.62) pertain to spiritual awakening and carrying the message of recovery.

Sobriety Stories The sobriety story is a three-part story that alcoholics tell of their defeat, surrender, and recovery. These stories can trigger a conversion experience in active addicts who hear them. Part one is the drunkalogue, a chain of anecdotes illustrating the person's life before recovery. Part two describes the turning point, the moment when the drinker first experiences a conviction of powerlessness over alcohol. Part three is a gratitude song telling what the person is like now, working a recovery program. Mark's gospel is a third-person version of Jesus' recovery story.[9] Chapters one through twelve reflect Jesus' drunkalogue, and chapters thirteen and fourteen his turning point. Thereafter Mark could only hint at part three, since the expectations of his Christian audience compelled him to include a crucifixion narrative whereas the Markôs people likely believed that Jesus, sober at last, had been released after his arrest and had returned anonymously to Galilee.

Principles not Personalities Sobriety fellowships have no place for messiahs, overlords, or other kinds of leader figures. Alcoholics Anonymous has but one ultimate authority, God as he expresses himself in the group conscience. The anonymity of A.A. members is a reminder to put spiritual principles before personalities. Mark's references to Jesus as the Christ (Greek for Messiah) and as the Son of God (a synonym for Messiah) were necessary to satisfy his Christian audience, but Jesus' sayings display a studied ambiguity concerning Messiahship. Christian readers understand Jesus to be identifying himself as the Messiah, whereas the Markôs fellowship knew that he believed "Messiah" referred to the Messianic nature of the program he founded, and not to his person as founder.

Religion versus Spirituality Recovering people contrast religion and spirituality. Religions often practice drinking rituals and promote strife, self will, and submission to human authority, whereas spiritual recovery programs stress stopping drinking, surrender, and seeking direction from a Higher Power. Recovery is a benign anarchy wherein God rules directly whereas religions set up hierarchies of human rulers. Religion exalts the personages of its leaders whereas recovery considers the anonymity of all members a guarantor of spiritual wellbeing. It was these aspects of the religion of his day that aroused Jesus' anger and became the targets of his messianism.

Text and Apparatus

Sobriety Mark is an account of Jesus' career as Mark learned of it from fellow Markôs people and perhaps, years before, from Jesus himself. It is the version he would have written had it not been necessary to keep the real story secret. The translation of Sobriety Mark is layed out as follows:

Apparatus I have divided the gospel into six parts, each one (after Part I) introduced by a brief explanation of its function within the narrative as a whole. The parts are further divided into segments titled from the perspective of recovery. Each segment consists of: Sobriety Mark first; Christian Mark (Revised Standard Version) next, less verses identical in both translations; and notes at the end. One can read Sobriety Mark by itself, read it with the notes, compare Sobriety Mark with Christian Mark, or examine one segment at a time with the aid of a scholarly commentary on the gospel.

Direct translations of the Greek text are printed in roman. Material not in the Greek—glosses, explanations of reference and figure, and content omitted by ellipsis—is printed in italics. Ellipses (. . .) indicate places where Christian camouflage has been omitted from translation. The notes explain translational choices and material too involved to include in the running text. I have kept the notes as brief as possible consistent with the need to describe the linguistic basis of the readings.

Story Type Most alcoholics agree that recovery from addiction requires freedom from alcohol followed by freedom from self. Many recovering addicts following the Twelve Steps attain this goal without ado. Others more seriously beset by ego and related defects of character (I include myself here) have a difficult time stopping playing God and letting go of self. We act out our mental drunkenness and often drink again before hitting bottom a final time and getting sober for good. Jesus' story is of this second type. The story line is as follows:

a) A wine addict banished from his home, Jesus renounces wine for water (Jordan baptism and wilderness experience),

b) enjoys a honeymoon period carrying the Markôs message to others (Galilean ministry casting out wine demons, formulating the Twelve, and teaching about recovery),

c) increasingly plays God (anger at people's refusal to accept the Rule of God as Messianic, rejection of followers, contentious responses to criticism by religious figures, guru-like behavior, and decision to go to Jerusalem),

d) drinks again (entering Jerusalem on a donkey, that is to say, wine drunk),

e) commits acts of drunken violence (attempting to seize the drinking vessels of Temple worshipers) and verbal warfare (rhetorical attacks on the scribes and chief priests),

f) is sought for arrest,

g) experiences a hangover apocalypse (admonitions to watch for the moment one sees ritual drinking as "the abomination that makes desolation," 13.14),

h) recognizes that wine is his problem, offers the cup to others that they might experience the same recognition, and announces his decision to drink no more (Last Supper discourse),

i) prayerfully requests help in surrendering, admits his powerlessness before God, asks for removal of his addiction to the cup, and repudiates self will (prayer in Gethsemane),

j) asserts that Messiahship resides not in his person but in all recovering people empowered by God and coming and going in heavenly witness (statement to the Jerusalem high priest, 14.62; also in his hangover apocalypse, 13.26-27),

k) is recognized as a drunkard not an insurrectionist and therefore freed,

l) and finally returns to Galilee to live out a sober life ("I will go before you to Galilee," 14.28 echoed in 16.7), no longer an impostor Son of God but a son of man at last, a truly human being and and thus truly a child of God.

Types of Content The following kinds of material in Christian Mark are reconceived in Sobriety Mark:

Jesus' actions Christian Mark depicts Jesus as a Messiah engaged in rabbinical disputation with Galilean Pharisees on points of Torah, bemused by rejection, disappointed by the failure of the disciples' mission, committed to carry the Gospel to Jerusalem regardless of cost to himself, and righteously angered by corrupt Temple practices and the refusal of the Jerusalem authorities to respond to his efforts to correct their errant ways. Desanitized in Sobriety Mark, this material appears as evidence of Jesus' worsening drunkenness, mental and physical, en route to surrender—his grandiosity, judgmentalness, contentiousness, and violent acting out. This is not to defame Jesus but to rescue him from the projections of Christian perfectionism and show him as the exemplar of addicted humankind that he was, a gravely ill person whose suffering shows the way to graced wellness.

Displaced parables Certain materials originally spoken by Jesus as parables appear in Christian Mark as depictions of actual events, usually with miraculous overtones. In Sobriety Mark these materials are restored to parabolic form. Examples: feeding the multitudes, multiplication of bread, walking on water, calming stormy seas.

Sobriety emblems Numerous items of content, seemingly disjunct in Christian Mark, cohere in Sobriety Mark as emblems of recovery. Examples: "gospel" is translated wellness message or recovery proclamation; "Son of man" is anonymous recovering person, Jesus and/or others; disciples are Markôs people; bread is the word of recovery spoken in Markôs meetings; angels are ex-addicts acting as messengers of recovery; persons possessed by demons or unclean spirits are active alcoholics.

Restored ellipses Another device of Markan concealment is ellipsis, the omission of words or phrases either because they are known by the audience hence superfluous or, as in Mark's case, because the writer wishes to render meaning ambiguous or otherwise indeterminate. Examples from early in chapter one: as he raised up from . . . the water (1.10); the spirit . . . descending upon him (1.10); the spirit . . . drove him into the wilderness (1.12); proclaiming God's wellness message . . . (1.14). Sobriety Mark restores this elliptical material as follows: as he raised up from *drinking* the water; the spirit *of God* descending upon him; the spirit *of drink* drove him into the wilderness; proclaiming God's wellness message *to inebriates*. The restoration of ellipses is unnecessary when readers in the target and the original languages share the same interpretive assumptions. For Christian readers the illustrations just shown do not need their ellipses restored, since all Christians regardless of their language share the understanding that Jesus rose up from *immersion in* the water, that both instances of spirit were *of God*, and that the message was proclaimed *to everyone*. But when a text is believed to have originated in a group whose interpretive perspective differed from that of a subsequent audience, then the restoration of ellipses is an important part of the task of translation.

Parables The parables of the Rule of God are the same in Sobriety Mark as in Christian Mark.

Ambiguous episodes Important episodes are presented in Sobriety Mark in a way that reveals their connection to recovery. Examples: baptism, temptation in the wilderness, sermon on ego death, not telling about Messiahship, donkey-figtree-Temple, apocalyptic discourse, Last Supper, and Gethsemane.

Errant disciples In Sobriety Mark, Jesus turns his back on his principal followers because of their failure to understand about multiplication of bread, Messiah, the priority of service over authority, and Passover drinking. In the end, Mark portrays the disciples as ritual drinkers, prototypes of Christian clergy called to minister the Communion cup to the many as part of God's plan for the recovery of humanity.

Prophetic allegories Jesus' recovery story ends with his trial by the Jewish council. Markôs people knew that Jesus had been released unharmed, but Christian belief required Mark to depict a crucifixion. Thus he combined oral tradition and fictional elements to produce the scenarios with which his gospel ends, scenarios that Christians read as actual but that Cupmasters understood as prophetic allegories pointing to Christianity's betrayal, denial, and entombment of the real Jesus story.

Camouflage Certain material in the Greek text serves only to reinforce a Christian understanding of Jesus' career and thus to camouflage the hidden recovery story. This material is omitted or decamouflaged as follows:

Messiah titles and emblems Christ; Son of God; expressions of wonder from the crowds; transfiguration; Messianic trappings in the Jerusalem entry story; absolute "I am" to the high priest; centurion's profession.

Vocabulary of exorcism The nonrealistic exorcisms early in the gospel camouflage stories of addicts at the turning point whom

Jesus brought into recovery. These are decamouflaged as follows: Possessed persons are identified as drunkards. Their "Son of God" professions are omitted. Jesus' warnings to "tell no one" are admonitions to the newly sober to respect his anonymity and not publicize his feats.

Sayings In deference to Jesus' reputation as a sage, Mark includes two groups of sayings: inoffensive material characteristic of Jesus' teaching in Galilee (7.1-23), and extremist sayings reflecting his mental drunkenness en route to Jerusalem(9.42-10.12, 10.17-22). While the contrast between the two groups points to the deterioration of Jesus' spiritual condition, the sayings are omitted from Sobriety Mark.

Healings Despite the emphasis placed upon healing by the early Church, Markôs people knew that Jesus was not a healer. Mark links healing the sick with casting out demons in order to protect his camouflage, fearing that if he identified Jesus only as an exorcist, Christian readers focused solely on casting out demons might recognize what it really was, code for curing drunkards. All healings are omitted from Sobriety Mark except the following: The cure of the leper relates to Jesus' alcoholism. The stories of the woman with the twelve-year hemorrhage and the seemingly dead twelve-year-old girl illustrate the sinister nature of alcohol. And the three two-stage healing stories at the gospel's hinge (Canaanite woman, deaf and dumb man, blind man) parabolically signify the two stages of recovery.

Finally, I caution readers not to think of Sobriety Mark as meant to replace Christian Mark. The two are different gospels serving different purposes. Both are present in the Greek original, the result of Mark's intentional use of homonymity and other kinds of ambiguity. Homonyms vary from language to language, however, and translations of the two gospels will require different words to render their different meanings. For example, Mark knew that his Christian audience reading the baptism story (1.9-11) would understand the Greek *baptizō* as "dip a person into water as a purification ritual" while Markôs people would understand it as "dip liquid into a cup for drinking." But English lacks a word having both senses of *baptizō*; hence the English version of Sobriety Mark 1.9 will say something quite different from the

English of the same verse in Christian Mark. In short, the Greek Gospel of Mark is a single document containing two gospel texts, whose translation into any other language requires the production of two documents each containing a single gospel text.

Notes

1. Morton Smith, *Clement of Alexandria and a Secret Gospel of Mark* (Cambridge, Mass.: Harvard University Press, 1973). A portion of Secret Mark is quoted below, p. 110.

2. The Anti-Marcionite Prologue, a late second-century document by an unknown writer, speaks of "[Mark] who is called 'stump-fingered' because he had rather small fingers in comparison with the rest of his body." The explanation of the name is so obvious as to suggest that the writer of the Prologue did not know its real meaning.

3. Martin Hengel, *Studies in the Gospel of Mark*, trans. John Bowden (Philadelphia: Fortress Press, 1985) 50-53, reviews the evidence of Mark's connection to Peter in Rome.

4. Mark's fears were not immediately realized. Although the Temple was destroyed in 70 A.D., the dispersion of the populace did not occur until the second Roman-Jewish War in 135 A.D.

5. Jewish Christians (Nazarenes) were numerous enough by the end of the century that the Twelfth Benediction of the synagogue service prayed God's wrath upon them, along with heretics and the Roman occupiers.

6. The Babylonian Talmud, Baba Batra 60b, states that after the Temple was destroyed, ascetics who would not eat meat or drink wine multiplied in Israel. Many of their number would have joined the Markôs groups seeking spiritual solace, unaware that their self-willed abstinence is incompatible with the spirituality that flows from powerlessness over alcohol.

7. This conjectural etymology comes from the Aramaic scholar Gustaf Dalman. See John C. Mellon, *Mark as Recovery Story* (Urbana, Ill.: University of Illinois Press, 1995) 279*n*33.

8. The material in this paragraph is documented in *Recovery Story*, 27-30 and 131-137.

9. A reconstruction of Jesus' story appears in *Recovery Story*, 150-154.

The Gospel of Mark

Prologue (1.1-8)

1 [1]The beginning of the recovery story of Jesus. . . . [2]As it is written in Isaiah the prophet, "Behold, I send my messenger before your face, who shall prepare your way; [3]the voice of one crying in the wilderness: Prepare the way of the Lord, make his paths straight." [4]John the baptizer appeared in the wilderness, preaching a baptism of repentance for the remission of sins. [5]And there went out to him all the country of Judea, and all the people of Jerusalem; and they were baptized by him in the river Jordan, confessing their sins. [6]Now John was clothed with camel's hair, and had a leather girdle around his waist, and ate locusts and wild honey. [7]And he preached, saying, "After me comes he who is mightier than I, the thong of whose sandals I am not worthy to stoop down and untie. [8]I have baptized you with water; but he will baptize you in a sanctifying spirit."

Revised Standard Version (RSV): [1]The beginning of the gospel of Jesus Christ, the Son of God. 2-8 *Ibid.* [8]. . . with the Holy Spirit.

Notes: **Recovery story** in Sobriety Mark renders the Greek *euangelion*, literally, wellness message. The titles "Christ" and "Son of God" are Messianic camouflage, hence omitted. Markôs people would have seen in the **prologue** a series of stage-two members of stage-one/stage-two pairs signifying that the gospel recounts the second stage of Jesus' recovery, not the first; not his Galilean "honeymoon" but his ultimate recovery in Jerusalem. The stage-two nature of this material becomes apparent when each element of the prologue is characterized in terms of contrastive foci: not John the Baptist who came first, but Jesus who came second; not first Isaiah but second Isaiah; not the earlier Egyptian captivity but the later Babylonian; not first knowledge but after knowledge (*metanoia*, here translated repentance); not water baptism, which initiates recovery, but spiritual baptism, which culminates it.

PART I: HONEYMOON

Sobering Up (1.9-13)

[9]In those days Jesus, *banished for drunkenness* from Nazareth in Galilee, came and was *told* by John to dip from the Jordan. [10]And just as he raised up from *drinking* the water, he sensed the heavens tearing apart and the spirit *of God* descending upon him . . . [11]and a voice coming from heaven, "You are my beloved son; with you I am well pleased." [12]At once the spirit *of drink* drove him into the wilderness [13]for forty days of *withdrawal cravings*, and Satan tempted him *to rely on willpower instead of God to stay sober.* He saw the wild beasts *of delirium,* but *sobriety* messengers ministered to him.

---

[9]In those days Jesus came from Nazareth of Galilee and was baptized by John in the Jordan. [10]And when he came up out of the water, immediately he saw the heavens opened and the Spirit descending upon him like a dove; 11-13 *Ibid.* [13]. . . tempted by Satan; and he was with the wild beasts; and the angels ministered to him.

Notes: The restored ellipsis **banished for drunkenness** makes explicit the alcoholism context. It reflects Jesus' identification as "a glutton and drunkard" in Mt 11.19/Lk 7.34, from Dt 21.20 wherein the phrase is better translated "unbridled drunkard" or "fullblown alcoholic."[1]

Told to dip from the Jordan: the Greek *baptizō* (baptize) is the first instance of an important lexical ambiguity in Mark. Literally it meant to dip, but its different senses were (a) to dip fabric in a dye solution, (b) to dip a person into water as a purification rite, (c) to dip liquid from a larger vessel into a cup for drinking, and (d) figuratively, to undergo a trial or ordeal. Hearers had to infer from context which sense of "dip" the speaker intended. In ministering to drunkards, John would have told them that from now on they should dip water instead of wine. Hence the restored ellipsis, **raised up from drinking the water.**

Tearing apart, from *schizō*, to tear assunder or rip violently, describes a psychic event, the cataclysmic breakup of established patterns of thinking that occurs with the advent of sobriety. "Like a dove" omitted as Messianic. **Beloved son**: a part of Jesus' new way of thinking. Ps 116 promises sonship (verse 16) to all who admit powerlessness before God (verse 10). *Mark as Recovery Story* examines this psalm, implicitly referred to in Mk 14.26 as part of the Hallel which Jesus and the disciples sang at the conclusion of the Last Supper.[2]

Spirit of God/of drink: "spirit" contains an ambiguity which turns on an implicit Latinism in Mark's Greek, *spiritus* as meaning both God (its first use here) and the intoxicating element in wine (its second use). **Drove him**: *ekballō*, to drive out violently, said of demons. Considered odd when said of spirit as God, the word appropriately describes the action of spirit as alcohol. Here is the first occasion on which an item traditionally considered puzzling or anomalous is explained by the alcoholism reading. The Markans knew that **the wilderness** referred to Jesus' difficult detoxification. **Satan**, literally "adversary," is the alcoholic ego tempting the drinker to return to self-empowerment, **willpower**, as a means of staying dry. **Wild beasts**: Markan code for *delirium tremens.* **Messengers**: *angeloi*, literally "message bearers," were John's disciples carrying the message of sobriety to Jesus as he dried out, "twelfth-stepping him" in today's A.A. parlance.

Proclaiming the Message (1.14-20)

[14]Now after John was arrested, Jesus came into Galilee proclaiming God's wellness message *to inebriates*, [15]saying, "The time is fulfilled and the Rule of God is at hand; change your mind and trust the wellness message." [16]And passing along by the Sea of Galilee he saw *two fellow drinkers*, Simon and Andrew the brother of Simon, casting a net in the sea; for they were fishermen. [17]And Jesus said to them, "Follow me and I will make you fishers of men." [18]And immediately they left their nets and followed him. [19]And going on a little farther he saw *two others*, James the son of Zebedee and John his brother, who were in their boat mending the nets. [20]And as soon as he called them, they left their father Zebedee in the boat with the hired servants, and followed him.

---

[14]Now after John was arrested, Jesus came into Galilee, preaching

the gospel of God, [15]saying, "The time is fulfilled, and the kingdom of God is at hand; repent and believe in the gospel." 1.16-20 *Ibid.*

Notes: John's arrest prompted Jesus to begin proclaiming recovery on his own. Enthused by sobriety, Jesus returned to Galilee to carry the **wellness message** ("gospel" in Christian Mark) to fellow addicts. Jesus learned early the timeless truth of sobriety: you keep it by giving it away. **Rule of God**, *Basileia tou Theou*, a term new to Jewish religious literature, was the name Jesus coined for the Markôs program. Most translations render *basileia* as kingdom, but the Greek term may be presumed to translate Jesus' original Aramaic *malkuta*, which lacked the spatial meaning of kingdom and conveyed only the sense of a time of ruling or reigning. Alcoholics today say that A.A. is not a thing or a place, it is letting God be God. So too with the Rule of God.

Change your mind translates *metanoia* etymologically as the "after knowledge" of recovery rather than as a religious repentance. **Trust** looks behind the Greek *pistueō* to the Aramaic *hemin*, which refers not to doctrinal belief but to crisis belief, belief enacted in other-trusting action. The four **fishermen** beheld in Jesus something they wanted, and their metanoia illustrates another important principle of Twelve-Step thinking: recovery works by attraction not promotion. Their unconditional response highlights the priority of sobriety over familial and vocational ties. **Fishers of men** puns with fishermen and promises newcomers that the day will come when they too will bring drinkers into recovery. Thus began Jesus' sobriety honeymoon in Galilee.

Sobriety in the Synagogue (1.21-28)

[21]And they went into Capernaum; and immediately on the sabbath he entered the synagogue and taught *those addicted to religious drinking the truth about their illness*. [22]And they were astonished at his teaching, for he taught them as one who had authority, and not as the scribes. [23]Suddenly up came a man with a wine demon. [24]He cried out, "We have nothing to do with you, Jesus of Nazareth. You've come to ruin our drinking, have you? I know who you are! . . ." [25]But Jesus rebuked him, saying, "Be quiet, and let go of your addiction!" [26]Convulsing drunkenly, the man cried out with

a loud voice *confessing his inebriety*. [27]And they were amazed and full of questioning . . . that the wine demons should obey him. [28]And at once word went out about him in that region of Galilee.

21-23 *Ibid.* except 23, man with an unclean spirit. [24]and he cried out, "What have you to do with us, Jesus of Nazareth? Have you come to destroy us? I know who you are, the Holy One of God." [25]". . . and come out of him." [26]And the unclean spirit, convulsing him and crying out with a loud voice, came out of him. [27] . . . so that they questioned among themselves, saying, "What is this? A new teaching! With authority he commands even the unclean spirits, and they obey him."

Notes: Casting out **demons** and **unclean spirits** (synonyms in Mark) is Markôs code for bringing drunkards to admit their illness, the first step towards recovery. **The synagogue**: for Jesus, **religious drinking** was as much a symptom of addiction as was chronic drunkenness. This was what he **taught**, unidentified in Christian Mark. Later his attack on wine vessels in the Temple and his disavowal of Passover drinking at the Last Supper will also target religious drinking. It is no accident, then, that his first contact with the wine demon occurs in the synagogue, where the wine of Kiddush is drunk. The demon is a personification of the man's illness and not a separate being. Like all defiant drinkers, the man's **we have nothing to do with you** denies any connection to Jesus' message; see I Sam 16.10 and Jn 2.4 for other instances of the Hebrew expression of disavowal behind the Greek. Yet his time has come, and his **loud cry** following his alcoholic **convulsion** is a gut-wrenching admission of addictive drinking blurted out after long denial. Many an alcoholic remembers such a moment in their own turning-point experience. **Holy One of God** is omitted as Messianic, as is all of verse 27.

Anonymity (1.32-39)

[32]In the evening, at sundown, they brought to him all who were possessed by the wine demon. [34]And he brought many thus possessed into recovery. And he tried to prevent the newly sober from saying that they knew him, *violating his anonymity by extolling him personally*. [35]And in the morning,

a great while before light, he rose and went out to a lonely place, and there he prayed *for help to stay sober that day.* [36]And Simon and those who were with him followed him, [37]and they found him and said to him, "Everyone is searching for you." [38]And he said to them, "Let us go on to the next towns, that I may proclaim there also; for that is why I came out." [39]And he went throughout all Galilee, proclaiming *sobriety* in their synagogues and curing drunkards.

---

[32] . . . brought to him all who were sick or possessed with a demon. [33]And the whole city was gathered together about the door. [34]And he healed many who were sick with various diseases, and cast out many demons; and he would not permit the demons to speak, because they knew him. 35-38 *Ibid.* [39]And he went throughout all Galilee, preaching in their synagogues and casting out demons.

References to healing the sick are Markan inventions to keep the Christian audience from focusing on casting out demons as the sole target of Jesus' work and guessing its actual meaning. Hence the omission of RSV's "all who were sick" and "sick with various diseases." Verse 33 is omitted as Messianic hyperbole. **In the evening**: recovery meetings usually occur at night, when alcoholics are most susceptible to drink. Because Jesus, like A.A. members today, believed that notoriety would focus attention on him and away from the principles of sobriety, he sought to remain anonymous. **Tried to prevent** is a realistic and non-Messianic translation of "would not permit." **That they knew him**: often considered a problem when rendered "because," *hoti* as "that" points to what Jesus wanted addicts not to say. **Breaking his anonymity**: noising his name and mission about. **Curing drunkards**: uncamouflaged version of "casting out demons." RSV's "preaching in their synagogues and casting out demons" is a telling instance wherein Mark does not bother to mention healing along with casting out. The entire passage shows Jesus remaining faithful to the single purpose of his mission (proclaiming sobriety), observing the principle of anonymity (telling the newly sober to focus on spiritual principles rather than his personal reputation) and working his own program (morning prayer for daily help).

Distractions (1.29-31, 40-45)

[29]And immediately he left the synagogue, and entered the house of Simon and Andrew, with James and John. [30]Now Simon's mother-in-law lay sick with a fever, and immediately they told him of her. [31]And he came and took her by the hand and lifted her up, and the fever left her; and she served them.

[40]And a leper came to him beseeching, and kneeling said to him, "If you will, you can make me clean." [41]Although angered, Jesus stretched out his hand and touched him, and said to him, "I will; be clean." [42]And immediately the leprosy left him, and he was made clean. [43]And Jesus sternly charged him, and sent him away at once, [44]and said to him, "See that you say nothing to anyone; but go, show yourself to the priest, and offer for your cleansing what Moses commanded, for a proof to the people." [45]But he went out and began to talk freely about it, and to spread the news, so that Jesus could no longer openly enter a town, but remained in desert places; and people came to him from every quarter.

29-31 and 40-45 *Ibid.* but "moved with pity," not "angered," in 41.

Notes: The episode involving Peter's mother-in-law, who when greeted by Jesus shakes off her fever and resumes her womanly work, portrays Jesus' initial realization that his charism might extend beyond working with addicts, that he might also succeed in other kinds of faith healing. The episode with the leper shows Jesus for the first time overtly acting out the role of healer, saying: **I will; be clean**. Whatever the man's actual ailment, he believes himself cured. Jesus wisely tells him to keep quiet about the incident, but he bruits it about. Jesus is gravely conflicted here, as shown by **angered**, from *orgizō*, to arouse to anger, found in certain manuscripts instead of "moved with pity" and thought by some scholars to be the preferred reading. Increasingly fascinated by his appeal to ill and afflicted persons other than addicts, yet concerned that fame and a broadening of his activity will compromise the effectiveness of his alcoholism movement, Jesus experiences the negative emotion conveyed by *orgizō*. The seeds of Jesus' mental drunkenness have yet to be planted, but the soil in which they will grow is cultivated by the incidents reported here.

First Conflict (2.1-12)

2 [1]And when he returned to Capernaum after some days, it was reported that he was at a certain house. [2]And many were gathered together, so that there was no longer room for them, not even about the door; and he was telling them about recovery. [3]And they came bringing to him a man paralyzed *by drink* carried by four men. [4]And when they could not get near him because of the crowd, they removed the roof above him; and when they had made an opening, they let down the pallet on which the drunken man lay. [5]And when Jesus saw their faith *act*, he said to the inebriate, "My son, your error is forgiven." [6]Now some scribes sitting there questioned in their hearts, [7]"Why does this man speak thus? It is blasphemy! Who can forgive sins but God alone?" [8]Then Jesus, perceiving in his spirit that they thus questioned within themselves, said to them, "Why do you question thus in your hearts? [9]Which is easier, to say to this drunkard, 'Your sins are forgiven,' or to say, 'Rise, take up your pallet and walk'? [10]But so you may know that recovering people have authority on earth to forgive error"—he said to the drunken man—[11]"I say to you, rise, take up your pallet, and go home." [12]And he rose, and immediately took up the pallet and went out before them all.

1-12a *Ibid.* [1]at home. [10]the Son of man. [12b]so that they were all amazed and glorified God, saying, "We never saw anything like this!"

Notes: **Paralyzed by drink** translates *paralutikos*, from *paraluein*, to loose or disable, a word with multiple meanings ranging from neurological disorder to stupor and bodily collapse resulting from drinking undiluted wine.[3] "Paralyzed" was drunkenness slang in the ancient world just as in modern times. **Your error is forgiven** roughly equates to the reassurance given A.A. newcomers today, "You're not a bad person, you're a sick person." Jesus' disputation with the scribes ends with his call to the drunken man to rally himself and arise, which he does. **Recovering people**, "son of man" in RSV, is a proper noun in Christian Mark referring solely to Jesus as Messiah, whereas in Sobriety Mark it is an indefinite noun collectively referring to Jesus and other Markôs people.[4] Even though he behaves soberly enough throughout the exchange, Jesus here begins a conflict with religious authorities that before long will end his sobriety honeymoon.

Illness As Desideratum (2.13-17)

[13]He went out again beside the sea; and all the crowd gathered about him, and he taught them. [14]And as he passed on, he saw Levi the son of Alphaeus sitting at the tax office, and he said to him, "Follow me." And he rose and followed him. [15]And Jesus sat *in a Markôs meeting* in the home where he was, and many tax collectors and sinners were numbered among his fellow alcoholics; for there were many who followed him. [16]And the scribes, when they saw that he was meeting with sinners and tax collectors, said to his followers, "Why does he meet with tax collectors and sinners?" [17]And when Jesus heard it, he said to them, "Able people have no need of a healer, but those who are sick . . . ."

13-14 *Ibid.* [15]And as he sat at table in his house, many tax collectors and sinners were sitting with Jesus and his disciples; for there were many who followed him. [16]And the scribes, when they saw that he was eating with sinners and tax collectors, said to his disciples, "Why does he meet with tax collectors and sinners?" [17]And when Jesus heard it, he said to them, "Those who are well have no need of a physician, but those who are sick; I came not to call the righteous, but sinners."

Notes: **Beside the sea/at home**: Mark alternates the settings of his Jesus anecdotes between public gatherings outdoors and indoor Markôs meetings. The difference is similar to that between open and closed A.A. meetings. **Sat in a Markôs meeting** replaces "sat at table;" table fellowship in the Markan text is code for recovery meetings. **Tax**

collectors and sinners: religious observance and clean/unclean rules are irrelevant to membership in recovery, whose only requirement, in Jesus' day and now, is a desire to stop drinking. **Fellow alcoholics**: *mathētais*, "disciples" in RSV, is code for Markôs people, fellow recovering addicts. **Meeting with**: "eating" is code for holding a recovery meeting. **Why does he meet with**: here Mark edits the stock phrase "eat and drink" and mentions only eating, since Cupmasters no longer drink. **Able people**: *ischuontes*, usually translated "those who are well," literally means strong or mighty. Jesus surely believed that all are needy before God, and by "able" presumably meant persons laboring under the illusion of auto-empowerment, a chief symptom of addiction, whether active or latent. The aphorism in 17a contains the implication of illness as desideratum and its recognition as fortuity, a key paradox of recovery. 17b, "not the righteous but sinners," is omitted as a post-Mark redaction aimed at refocusing Jesus' message from illness to sin.

New Wine (2.18-22)

[18]Now John's disciples and the Pharisees were fasting; and people came and said to him, "Why do John's disciples and the disciples of the Pharisees fast, but your disciples do not fast?" [19]And Jesus said to them, "Can the wedding guests fast while the bridegroom is with them? As long as they have the bridegroom with them, they cannot fast. . . . [21]No one sews a piece of unshrunk cloth on an old garment; if he does, the patch tears away from it, the new from the old, and a worse tear is made. [22]And no one puts new wine into old wineskins; if he does, the wine will burst the skins, and the wine is lost, and so are the skins; but new wine is for fresh skins."

18-19 and 21-22 *Ibid.* [20]The days will come, when the bridegroom is taken away from them, and then they will fast in that day.

Notes: **Bridegroom** is a parabolic figure based on the stereotypical image of the wedding celebration as the epitome of earthly joy. To Christians, bridegroom was a metaphor for Messiah, but to the Markôs people it symbolized the joy of new life in sobriety. Verse 20 is omitted as a post-

Mark addition by Church redactors. The two parables of **unshrunk cloth** and **new wine** point to the incompatibility of Markôs spirituality and the inflexible rules and mandated fasting of religion. The point of the parables is clear: mixing religion and recovery undermines both.

Omitted Non-Markôs Material (2.23-3.10)

Most of this omitted material pertains to an issue of importance to Jewish Christians, namely, the status of sabbath regulations in the new religion. Apparently the stories of harvesting grain for immediate consumption (2.23-28) and doing a work of healing (3.1-6) on the sabbath are intended to show that Jesus liberalized sabbath restrictions without repudiating them outright. The material in 3.7-10 is Messianic.

Formulating the Twelve (3.11-19)

3 [11]And whenever they saw him, drunkards were attracted to him and called out *for help.* [12]And he strictly ordered them not to violate his anonymity. [13]And he went up into the hills, and called to him those whom he had in mind; and they came to him. [14]And he formulated twelve formulations to have with him, to be disseminated to announce/demonstrate [15]an authoritative/effective cure for wine addicts. . . .

---

[11]And whenever the unclean spirits beheld him, they fell down before him and cried out, "You are the Son of God." [12]And he strictly ordered them not to make him known. [13]And he went up into the hills, and called to him those whom he desired; and they came to him. [14]And he appointed twelve, to be with him, and to be sent out to preach [15]and have authority to cast out demons: [16]Simon whom he surnamed Peter; [17]James the son of Zebedee and John the brother of James, whom he surnamed Boanerges, that is, sons of thunder; [18]Andrew, and Philip, and Bartholomew, and Matthew, and Thomas, and James the son of Alphaeus, and Thaddaeus, and Simon the Cananaean, [19]and Judas Iscariot, who betrayed him.

Notes: **Were attracted to him**: *prospiptō*, to fall or move towards (also 5.33 and 7.25). Markôs people knew that the term conveyed the pull of sobriety on addicts at the turning point. **Called out for help**: the faith action that initiates recovery. "Son of God" is Messianic camouflage. **Called to him**, *proskaleō*, to call aside to oneself, denotes teaching imparted in what A.A. members would call a closed meeting. **Those whom he had in mind**: former addicts.

The conclusion of this surprising passage tells how Jesus formulated twelve precepts of sobriety for use by Markôs people. **Formulated twelve formulations**: An important lexical ambiguity, *poieō* means to appoint or ordain when said of persons, or to construct or formulate when said of things. Mark's use of "twelve" without a following noun leaves the reading open: appointed twelve appointees (Christian Mark) or formulated twelve formulations (Sobriety Mark). Contributing to the dual readings is the ambiguity of *apostellō*, to send out or to disseminate, and of *kērussō*, to preach or to announce/demonstrate. Functionally, the Twelve that Jesus formulated would have been similar to the Twelve Steps of A.A. *Mark as Recovery Story* speculates about the content of the Twelve, which probably was secret matter known only by Cupmasters.[5] The list of names (16-19) is camouflage intended to reinforce the Christian belief that Twelve referred to persons.

"He's Drunk Again" (3.20-35)

[20]Then he went home; and the crowd assembled again to prevent them from holding their Markôs meeting. [21]And when his family heard *the commotion*, they went out to seize him, for they said, "He's drunk again." [22]And the scribes who came down from Jerusalem said, "He is totally inebriated, and in his drunkenness he thinks to cure other inebriates." [23]And he called *his followers* to him and said to them in parables, "How can Satan cast out Satan? [24]If a kingdom is divided against itself, that kingdom cannot stand. [25]And if a house is divided against itself, that house will not be able to stand. . . . [27]But no one can enter a strong man's house and plunder his goods, unless he first binds the strong man; then indeed he may plunder his house. [28]Truly I say to you, all wrongs will be forgiven the sons of men, and whatever blasphemies they utter; [29]but whoever blasphemes against

the spirit of sanctification never has forgiveness, but is guilty of an eternal error. . . ." [31]And his mother and his brothers came; and standing outside they sent to him and called him. [32]And a crowd was sitting about him; and they said to him, "Your mother and your brothers are outside asking for you." [33]And he replied, "Who are my mother and my brothers?" [34]And looking around on those who sat about him, he said, "Here are my mother and my brothers! . . ."

20-21 *Ibid.* [22]And the scribes who came down from Jerusalem said, "He is possessed by Beelzebul, and by the prince of demons he casts out the demons." 23-25 *Ibid.* [26]And if Satan has risen up against himself and is divided, he cannot stand, but is coming to an end. 27-29 *Ibid.* [30]For they had said, "He has an unclean spirit." 31-34 *Ibid.* [35]"Whoever does the will of God is my brother, and sister, and mother."

Notes: Outraged to see a banished man return in the company of other drunkards, the Nazareth townspeople raise such a ruckus that Jesus and his followers are unable to hold the public meeting with which their work in each new town began. **Prevent them from holding their Markôs meeting**: again, "eat bread" is code for sharing the word of recovery in meetings. **Drunk again**: Jesus' family hear the commotion and, thinking him intoxicated again, come out to restrain him. Greek *existēmi*, translated "beside himself" in RSV, also means possessed or not sober. It is Mark's generic term for whatever Aramaic drunkenness idiom the family actually used. The anecdote has always embarrassed Christian interpreters including Matthew and Luke, who omit it entirely from their gospels.

The **scribes from Jerusalem** also think Jesus drunk, and their remark, stripped of the camouflage of demonology, derides him as a would-be rescuer of drunkards who is drunk himself. Thereafter, Jesus' parables (**Satan versus Satan, house divided, strong man**) assure his group that drunk drunks cannot sober up other drunk drunks. Verse 29, the "unforgivable sin" against the Holy Spirit, simply means that recovery won't work for those who deny that they can get better, that is, who deny **the spirit of sanctification** ("holy spirit"). In verse 34 Jesus assigns his program higher priority than family; for without it, as Jesus learned, persons lose their families. Exactly the same statement of priorities is often voiced in A.A. meetings today.

Secret of the Rule of God (4.10-12)

4 [10]And when he was alone, those who were around him who had gotten the twelve *precepts of sobriety* asked him concerning the parables. [11]And he said to them, "To you has been given the secret of the Rule of God, but for those still outside, everything must be in parables. . . ."

---

[10]And when he was alone, those who were around him with the twelve asked him concerning the parables. 11 *Ibid.* [12]". . . so that they may indeed see but not perceive, and may indeed hear but not understand; lest they should turn again, and be forgiven."

Notes: **Had gotten** translates the ambiguous *sun*, "with," in its possessive sense (meaning "have"), whereas Christian readers select the associative sense of "with" (meaning "and")—another ambiguity conveying different messages to different audiences. The idea of the sobriety version is that of owned knowledge or acquired understanding. Alcoholics today often speak about "getting" the Twelve Steps, that is, grasping them intuitively and in practice, and making them a part of one's daily living. Jesus is saying that an insider's metanoetic understanding of **the twelve precepts of sobriety**, the secret of the Rule of God, is something that can only be communicated parabolically to outsiders. Verse 12, while appropriate in its irony to both gospels, is omitted as an Old Testament prophecy fulfillment introduced into Christian Mark for its Messianic value.

Parables (4.1-9, 21-34)

[1]Again he began to teach beside the sea. And a very large crowd gathered about him, so that he got into a boat and sat in it on the sea; and the whole crowd was beside the sea on the land. [2]And he taught them many things in parables, and in his teaching he said to them: [3]"Listen! A sower went out to sow. [4]And as he sowed, some seed fell along the path, and the birds came and devoured it. [5]Other seed fell on rocky ground, where it had not much soil, and immediately it sprang up, since it had no depth of soil; [6]and

when the sun rose it was scorched, and since it had no root it withered away. [7]Other seed fell among thorns and the thorns grew up and choked it, and it yielded no grain. [8]And other seeds fell into good soil and brought forth grain, growing up and increasing and yielding thirtyfold and sixtyfold and a hundredfold." [9]And he said, "He who has ears to hear, let him hear.". . . [21]And he said to them, "Is a lamp brought in to be put under a bushel, or under a bed, and not on a stand? [22]For there is nothing hid, except to be made manifest; nor is anything secret except to come to light. [23]If any man has ears to hear, let him hear." [24]And he said to them, "Take heed what you hear; the measure you give will be the measure you get, and still more will be given you. [25]For to him who has will more be given; and from him who has not, even what he has will be taken away." [26]And he said, "The rule of God is as if a man should scatter seed upon the ground, [27]and should sleep and rise night and day, and the seed should sprout and grow, and he knows not how. [28]The earth produces of itself, first the blade, then the ear, then the full grain in the ear. [29]But when the grain is ripe, at once he puts in the sickle, because the harvest has come." [30]And he said, "With what can we compare the rule of God, or what parable shall we use for it? [31]It is like a grain of mustard seed, which, when sown upon the ground, is the smallest of all the seeds on earth; [32]yet when it is sown it grows up and becomes the greatest of all shrubs, and puts forth branches, so that the birds of the air can make nests in its shade. . . ."

1-9 *Ibid.* 21-32 *Ibid.* [33]With many such parables he spoke the word to them, as they were able to hear it; [34]he did not speak to them without a parable, but privately to his own disciples he explained everything.

Notes: The **parable of the sower** reflects the broadcast sowing of seed, wherein it is futile for the sower to concern himself about where the seed falls because the ground is such that it is impossible for him to place the grains in certain spots. He is not to judge but to trust that the wheat that should grow will. A parable about twelfth-stepping, it means carry the message and leave the results to God: some will not get it at all, some only for a time, and some to varying degrees of fullness. Verses 13-20 are omitted as Christian explication. The **parable of the lamp meant to shine** indicates that the good intended for persons will show forth in time. Good things still hidden will be revealed in due course, and our problems and misfortunes will be seen as what we had to go through to attain sobriety. The **parable of the seed growing in secret** will remind alcoholics of a past incident or chance encounter somehow linked to recovery, which they later refer to as "the moment the seed was planted," even though they had no inkling from then until their turning point that the message was growing within them. The **parable of the small seed/large shrub** means that the size of a movement's beginning is no indicator of its destined magnitude, whether in the inner life of one person or the outer life of an organization on the world stage.

Serenity Parable (4.35-41)

[35]On that day, when evening had come, he said to them, "Let us go across to the other side." [36]And leaving the crowd, they took him with them, just as he was, in the boat. And other boats were with him. [37-38]*And he said, "The Rule of God is like* a man cushioned and asleep in the stern of a boat. When a storm of wind arises, and waves beat into the boat and the boat begins to fill with water, [39]he awakes and rebukes the wind and the sea, and says, 'Peace! Be still!' And the wind ceases and a great calm comes." [40]He said to them, *"With faith, fear gives way to peace."*. . .

---

[35]On that day, when evening had come, he said to them, "Let us go across to the other side." [36]And leaving the crowd, they took him with them, just as he was, in the boat. And other boats were with him. [37]And a great storm of wind arose, and the waves beat into the boat, so that the boat was already filling. [38]But he was in the stern, asleep on the cushion; and they woke him and said to him, "Teacher, do you not care if we perish?" [39]And he awoke and rebuked the wind, and said to the

sea, "Peace! Be still!" And the wind ceased, and there was a great calm. [40]He said to them, "Why are you afraid? Have you no faith?" [41]And they were filled with awe, and they said to one another, "Who then is this, that even wind and sea obey him?"

Notes: This is the first of several serenity parables which Mark was compelled to recast as narratives depicting Jesus as a wonderworker capable of intervening in the natural order. The story does not reflect an actual storm at sea but the way persons in the Rule of God deal with situations that threaten their serenity. Both the narrative and the parabolic versions point to the interplay of **fear, faith**, and **peace**—the former through a focus on the person of Jesus, the latter through an emphasis on spiritual principles. Several other parables in addition to this one (Gerasene demoniac, walking on water, feeding the multitudes) had undergone similar narrative transformations, with the result that Jesus' reputation as a miracle worker had become a fixture of the Christian oral tradition. **Go across to the other side** may be a metaphorical invitation to shift one's thinking from the material to the spiritual. Otherwise, the parable speaks for itself.

Parable of Addiction (5.1-20)

5 [1]They came to the other side of the sea, to the country of the Gerasenes. [2]And when he came out of the boat, Jesus said, "Drunkards are like madmen [3]living among tombs, who cannot be governed, even with chains. [4]For when people try to govern them, they tear apart their chains and break their fetters; for people lack the power to bring them under rule. [5]Night and day, among the tombs and out on the mountains, they shout *in anger,* and hack each other to pieces with stones. [6]And when they see people coming, they obey the urging of drink [7]and shout, 'Your Most High God is none of our business! We swear by God, get off our backs! [9] . . . For we are legion, and there are many of us!'" [8]And Jesus said, "But when *a recovering person* comes and says, 'Let go of your addiction'. . . [15]then you will see these drunkards sitting *in meetings*, clothed and *sober*, . . . [18]and they will ask to go with us to cure other drunkards. [19]But first they must go home and witness to the grace of God, and *make amends* to their friends.". . .

---

[1]They came to the other side of the sea, to the country of the Gerasenes. [2]And when he had come out of the boat, there met him out of the tombs a man with an unclean spirit, [3]who lived among the tombs; and no one could bind him anymore, even with a chain; [4]for he had often been bound with fetters and chains, but the chains he wrenched apart; and the fetters he broke in pieces; and no one had the strength to subdue him. [5]Night and day among the tombs and on the mountains he was always crying out, and bruising himself with stones. [6]And when he saw Jesus from afar, he ran and worshiped him; [7]and crying out with a loud voice, he said, "What have you to do with me, Jesus, Son of the Most High God? I adjure you by God, do not torment me." [8]For he had said to him, "Come out of the man, you unclean spirit!" [9]And Jesus asked him, "What is your name?" He replied, "My name is Legion; for we are many." [10]And he begged him eagerly not to send them out of the country. [11]Now a great herd of swine was feeding there on the hillside; [12]and they begged him, "Send us into the swine, let us enter them." [13]So he gave them leave. And the unclean spirits came out and entered the swine; and the herd, numbering about two thousand, rushed down the steep bank into the sea, and were drowned in the sea. [14]The herdsmen fled, and told it in the city and in the country. And people came to see what it was that had happened. [15]And they came to Jesus, and saw the demoniac sitting there, clothed and in his right mind, the man who had had the legion; and they were afraid. [16]And those who had seen it told what had happened to the demoniac and to the swine. [17]And they began to beg Jesus to depart from their neighborhood. [18]And as he was getting into the boat, the man who had been possessed with demons begged him that he might be with him. [19]But he refused, and said to him, "Go home to your friends and tell them how much the Lord has done for you, and how he has had mercy on you." [20]And he went away and began to proclaim in the Decapolis how much Jesus had done for him; and all men marveled.

Notes: Cast as a folkloric narrative in Christian Mark, this parable begins by depicting the chaos caused by alcohol addiction in society, and ends with the victory of the Rule of God. The narrative presents one demoniac with many demons, while the parable in Sobriety Mark portrays one addiction shared by many addicts. **Tombs** is a place of outcast and death. **No longer be governed** points to the sociopathic behavior of addicts. **Shout in anger/hack to pieces** make it clear that addiction results in fighting and ultimately violent death. Verses 6, 7, and 9 show the addict's defiance of efforts by religion and religious people to get them off drink. **Legion** is a frightening metaphor suggesting that addicts collectively represent a challenge to the survival of civilization itself. Verses 8, 15, and 18 show the power of the Rule of God to turn addicts back into human beings. **Let go of your addiction** means change your mind (*metanoia*), admit your powerlessness, stop fighting, ask for help. **Witness to the grace of God** and reconciliation with **friends** may have been two of the Twelve sobriety precepts formulated by Jesus. Apparently the parable had already acquired the trappings of a bizarre folktale by the time it reached Mark, although his final version is a rather clumsy contrivance in which Jesus' first exorcism is uncharacteristically rebuffed (verse 8) and finally effected only after negotiation with the demons (verses 12-13). Rescued from folk narrative, the parable presents a comprehensive statement by Jesus on the evil of epidemic drunkenness. Its telling occurs just short of the high-water mark of Jesus' sobriety honeymoon.

Two Alcoholism Stories (5.21-43)

21And when Jesus had crossed again in the boat to the other side, a great crowd gathered about him; and he was beside the sea. 22Then came one of the rulers of the synagogue, Jairus by name; and seeing him he fell at his feet, 23and besought him, saying, "My little daughter is at the point of death. Come and lay your hands on her so that she may be made well, and live." 24And he went with him. And a great crowd followed him and thronged about him.

25And there was a woman *addict* who had had a flow of blood for twelve years, 26and who had suffered much under many physicians, and had spent all that she had *on their addictive potions*, and was no better but rather grew worse. 27She had heard the reports about Jesus, and came up behind him in the crowd and touched his garment. 28For she said, "If I touch even his garments, I shall be made well." [29]And immediately the hemorrhage ceased; and she felt in her body that she was healed of her disease. [30]And Jesus perceiving in himself that power had gone forth from him, immediately turned about in the crowd and said, "Who touched my garments?" [31]And his disciples said to him, "You see the crowd pressing around you, and yet you say, 'Who touched me?'" [32]And he looked around to see who had done it. [33]But the woman, fearful and trembling from her knowledge of what had happened to her, became drawn to him and told him the whole truth *about her addiction to medication*. [34]And he said to her, "Daughter, your faith has made you well; go in peace, and be healed of your illness."

[35]While he was still speaking, there came from the ruler's house some who said, "Your daughter is dead. Why trouble the teacher any further?" [36]But ignoring what they said, Jesus said to the ruler of the synagogue, "Do not fear, only believe." [37]And he allowed no one to follow him except Peter and James and John the brother of James. [38]When they came to the house of the ruler of the synagogue, he saw a tumult, and people weeping and wailing loudly. [39]And when he had entered, he said to them, "Why do you make a tumult and weep? The child is not dead but unconscious from wine." [40]And they laughed at him, but he put them all outside, and took the child's father and mother and those who were with him, and went in where the child was. [41]Taking her by the hand he said to her, "*Tal'itha cu'mi,*" which means, "Little girl, I say to you, snap out of it!" [42]And immediately the girl got up and walked; for she was twelve years old. . . . [43]And he strictly charged them that no one should know this, and told them to give her something to eat.

21-43 *Ibid.*, minus the italicized portions. [33]fell down before him. [39]not dead but sleeping. [41]I say to you, arise. 42 omitted, Messianic.

Notes: To complement the parable of the collective effect of drunkenness in human societies (Gerasene demoniac), Jesus recounts two quasi-parabolic anecdotes about the hiddenness of addiction. Presented in Christian Mark as a healing and a resurrection, the stories reflect occasions whereon Jesus recognized drink as the underlying problem in cases of a chronic physical affliction and an apparent death. The **woman addict** with a twelve-year hemorrhage suffered from variceal bleeding caused by medications laced with narcotics and primitively distilled alcohol. She had become, in effect, a "prescription junkie," and her addiction had perpetuated the bleeding. **Felt she was healed** reflects an awareness many recovering persons experience at the turning point. **Told the whole truth** may pertain to a stipulation in one of the Twelve. **Jairus's daughter**, in turn, exhibited symptoms of acute sensitivity to alcohol, presumably the wine she had drunk for the first time upon reaching **age twelve**. Perhaps it was uncut wine in her father's synagogue, drink consumed too eagerly in her first family ceremony, or the result of being plied by sibling pranksters—any number of familiar scenarios are readily imaginable. **Unconscious from wine**: "sleeping" in the Greek, obviously not meant literally, is a metaphor for her drunken stupor. To the alarm of her family, who truly thought her dead, she had passed out cold and came to only as the alcohol began to metabolize in her system. Persons so acutely allergic to drink generally avoid it thereafter, after such frightening initial experiences. Jesus' **strict charge** to her family is probably intended to shield her from ridicule. The two anecdotes do not label Jesus an anti-drink crusader, rather a recovering person who knows how deceptive and insidious alcohol can be. Placed at the acme of Jesus' honeymoon, the stories recount his last acts performed in the enthusiasm and pure joy of sobriety. From this point on, the alloy of mental drunkenness will more and more affect his actions.

PART II: MENTAL DRUNKENNESS

Sobriety Mark has five parts. Part one (chapters 1-5) depicts Jesus' honeymoon, how he sobers up, founds the Cupmaster (Markôs) fellowship and the program he calls the Rule of God, and formulates the Twelve sobriety precepts. Part two (chapters 6-8) shows the onset of mental drunkenness, beginning with Jesus' anger at his townsmen's refusal to accept the Messianic character of his movement. In part three (chapters 9-10) Jesus succumbs to messianism. Part four (chapters 11-12) shows his relapse and part five (chapters 13-14) his surrender and recovery.

The episode in the Nazareth synagogue (6.1-6) is pivotal. According to Luke's fuller account, Jesus announced the fulfillment of Isaiah's Messiah prophecy. Markôs people knew that it was the Rule of God, rather than himself, that Jesus had proclaimed as Messianic. At the same time, however, they believed he had spoken prematurely, failing to recognize the mental drunkenness that prompted his announcement. After all, their program was still in its infancy. Jesus had, in effect, ignored his own parables, claiming a harvest where there was only a sprout, calling a mustard seedling a grown shrub. Worse, in proclaiming the Rule of God wholesale to his fellow Jews rather than continuing to focus on drunkards, Jesus pits his recovery movement against religion in an oppositional, ultimately a combative, way. Why does he speak out? Known locally as a wine addict, humiliated earlier by his family, tensed by his ceremonial role in the synagogue, and derided by worshippers, Jesus succumbs to fear, anger, and hurt pride, classic symptoms of mental drunkenness. He reads the Messianic passage in Isaiah (61.1-2a) and announces, "Today this scripture has been fulfilled in your hearing" (Lk 4.21).

In the remainder of part two, Jesus rashly sends out his disciples and fulminates at their lack of success and continued inability to understand multiplication of bread as the central element of communal practice within the Cupmaster groups. Ultimately he turns his back on his followers and sets his face towards Jerusalem.

Anger Attack (6.1-6)

6 [1]He went away from there and came to his own country; and his disciples followed him. [2]And on the sabbath in the synagogue be began to teach *that the Rule of God fulfills the Isaian Messiah prophecy.* And many who heard him were greatly upset, saying, "Where did this man get all this? What is the wisdom given to him? What mighty works has he ever done, *beside drink*? [3]This is only the carpenter, the son of Mary and brother of James and Joses and Judas and Simon, and his sisters live here too." And they took offense at him. [4]Jesus said to them, "A prophet is not without honor, except in his own country, and among his own kin, and in his own house." [5]And he could do no mighty works there . . . . [6]And he raged at their unbelief.

1-4 *Ibid.* except 2, were astonished, saying. [5]And he could do no mighty works there, except that he layed his hands upon a few sick people and healed them. [6]And he marveled because of their unbelief.

Notes: **The Rule of God fulfills the Isaian Messiah prophecy**: this restored ellipsis derives from the assumption that Mark knew the fuller story of the episode in the Nazareth synagogue later included in Luke's gospel (4.16-30). Christian Mark omits the content of Jesus' teaching because the writer knew that his two audiences understood it differently. Christians believed that Jesus proclaimed himself Messiah, whereas Markôs people knew that it was the Rule of God, their alcoholism recovery program, that Jesus identified as Messianic. Either way, the people were **greatly upset** (*skandalizō*), and RSV's "astonished" is needlessly euphemistic. Unsure how Christians will respond, Mark omits not only the Isaian material but also the details of the altercation with the crowd subsequently reported by Luke, although he bluntly acknowledges Jesus' impotence on the occasion. **Beside drink** reflects the townspeople's derision heaped upon a man they knew as an incorrigible drunkard.

The reason Jesus **could do no mighty works**, however, is not his prior reputation but that the people recognized his actions here as fear-based and therefore withheld their faith. Their taunts angered him; *thaumazō*, **raged,** is an ambiguous verb of emotion translatable as positive or negative depending on its context. The Markans knew that Jesus was enraged. More to the point, they knew that the episode marked the end of his honeymoon and the onset of a mental drunkenness that would turn him away from helping drunkards and toward an unfocused messianism destined to govern his actions until the end. Jesus injects his recovery program into the arena of religious controversy, willfully proclaiming the Rule of God as the Messianic fulfillment of the ancient religion and thereby setting the stage for confrontation and violent conflict.

Misdirecting the Disciples (6.7-13, 30)

[7]And calling their attention to the Twelve *precepts of sobriety*, he began sending his followers out two by two, and gave them authority over wine demons, *and told them that they would be persecuted but that Messiah would appear before the end of their mission.* [8]He charged them to take nothing for their journey except a staff; no bread, no bag, no money in their belts; [9]but to wear sandals and not put on two tunics. [10]And he said to them, "Where you enter a house, stay there until you leave the place. [11]And if any place will not receive you and they refuse to hear you, when you leave, shake off the dust that is on your feet for a testimony against them." [12]So they went out and preached that men should change their minds, *and turn from their addictions, and accept the Rule of God.* [13]And they cured many drunkards . . . . [30]Those sent out returned to Jesus, and told him all that they had done and taught.

7-12 *Ibid.*, [7]called to him the twelve, . . . authority over the unclean spirits; [12]and preached that men should repent. [13]And they cast out many demons, and anointed with oil many that were sick and healed them.

Notes: To follow up his Messianic proclamation, Jesus commissions his disciples, armed with **the Twelve**, to announce the Rule of God in the surrounding towns. **Cured many drunkards** is the reality camouflaged by RSV's "casting out demons."

Here again, fearful of scandalizing his Christian audience by too graphically depicting Jesus' poor spiritual condition, Mark omits material, later reported by Matthew and Luke, symptomatic of Jesus' mental drunkenness. Matthew's account (10.5-23) of the instructions to the disciples includes Jesus' prediction **that they would be persecuted but that Messiah would appear before the end of their mission** (verse 7 above). The question is, what is the condition of a man who sends out bearers of good news, emissaries of a program of recovery and life, but predicts their persecution and rejection? The answer is, a man beset by fear, resentment, and self-will. Mark's unelaborated mention of the disciples' return indicates that they had nothing of moment to report—no persecutions, no Messianic theophany. Jesus was so angry that he cursed the towns visited by the disciples (Luke 10.13-15). Obviously, Jesus erred in sending out the disciples as he did. A century ago the famous scholar Albert Schweitzer saw this error as a crushing blow to Jesus. Instead of damping his mental drunkenness, however, it only increases his messianic obsession.

Omitted Material (6.14-29)

Between the sending out of the disciples (6.7-13) and their return (6.30), Mark includes material about Herod Antipater, tetrarch of Galilee, and about the death of John the Baptist, whom Herod beheaded at the request of his sister-in-law Herodius, who had a grudge against John. While the murder of John presumably contributed to Jesus' rising anger, this material serves mainly as an interlude between the sending out and the return, and is not a part of Sobriety Mark.

Parable of Meeting and Feeding (6.31-44)

[31]And Jesus said, "*Those in the Rule of God* draw apart by themselves alone and rest from time to time. For the many *on the outside* constantly come and go, and take no time to share the wisdom of recovery." [32]So they went away in the boat to a place by themselves alone. [33]Now the many saw them going, and knew them, and they ran there on foot from all the towns, and got there ahead of them. [34]As he landed he saw a great throng, and he had compassion on them, because they were like sheep without a shepherd; and he began to teach them *about sober living*. [35]And when it grew late, his disciples came to him and said, "This is a

lonely place, and the hour is now late; [36]send them away, to go into the country and the villages round about and buy themselves something to eat." [37]But he answered them, "You give them something to eat." And they said to him, "Shall we go and buy two hundred denarii worth of bread, and give it to them to eat?" [38]And he answered them *in a parable*, "The Rule of God is like a man who has a fullness of bread and fish wherewith to feed all who are present. [39-40]So he has the people recline as at table, sitting in groups. [41]And he takes the words of recovery like bread, and the actions enfleshed like fish, and he prays to God and speaks the wisdom to them all. *And the people by turns comment in their groups on what he has spoken.* [42]And so they feed and are fed, and all are satisfied. [43]And they take away from the meeting twelvefold, *a Messianic superabundance*." [44] . . .

---

[31]And he said to them, "Come away by yourselves to a lonely place, and rest a while." For many were coming and going, and they had no leisure even to eat. 33-37 *Ibid.* [38]And he said to them, "How many loaves have you? Go and see." And when they had found out, they said, "Five, and two fish." [39]Then he commanded them all to sit down by companies upon the green grass. [40]So they sat down in groups, by hundreds and by fifties. [41]And taking the five loaves and the two fish he looked up to heaven, and blessed, and broke the loaves, and gave them to the disciples to set before the people; and he divided the two fish among them all. [42]And they all ate and were satisfied. [43]And they took up twelve baskets full of broken pieces and of the fish. [44]And those who ate the loaves were five thousand men.

Notes: Sobriety Mark restores the story of the feeding of five thousand to its original form as a parable teaching that the words of recovery spoken in meetings, symbolized by bread, are not the leader's remarks alone but are multiplied by the comments of everyone present. A central parable in Jesus' teaching, it goes to the heart of Twelve-Step practice today. **Drawing apart alone** refers to Markôs meetings limited to alcoholics, like "closed meetings" in A.A. **Rest,** *anapauō*, in the Septuagint refers to sabbath rest, spiritual rest, the rest one finds in meetings. **On the outside** echoes "those outside" in 4.11, a reference to nonaddicts. **To share the wisdom of recovery**: "eating," *phagō*, is code for hearing the words of the Markôs program. **Sheep without a shepherd**, an implied criticism of religious officials, foreshadows Jesus' overt attack on clerical wrong-headedness in the third feeding parable (8.14-21). **A fullness of bread and fish**: 5 loaves plus 2 fish equals 7, symbol of completedness and perfection. **Recline as at table**, *anakeimai*, denotes the posture for banqueting and identifies recovery meetings as anticipations of the heavenly banquet. **Sitting in groups**: large A.A. meetings generally divide into groups for the comments. **They take away twelvefold**, "twelve baskets of broken bread and fish" in RSV, beautifully symbolizes how comments multiply the spiritual wisdom of recovery. **Twelve**, of course, is Messianic.

The point of the feeding parable is twofold. One, the "food" of recovery is words spoken in meetings, words that make ill people well, plus the actions of sober living which those words both reflect and counsel. Two, the genius of meetings is that it is not just the leader who speaks but the others present as well, who multiply the wisdom of the leader's words—the meeting lead, as A.A.s call it—by their individual follow-up comments sharing their experience, strength, and hope. It is the importance of these comments that the multiplication of bread points up. Mark represents the parable as a miracle and conceals the true meaning of the twelve-basket residue, not just to camouflage the Markôs practice of allowing all to speak but to satisfy the Jewish-Christian clergy of his own day, who believe that only they should be allowed to talk in their religious assemblies.

Second Serenity Parable (6.45-52)

[45]Immediately he made his disciples get into the boat and go before him to the other side, to Bethsaida, while he dismissed the crowd. [46]And after he had taken leave of them, he went into the hills to pray. [47]And when evening came, the boat was still at sea, and he was still on land. [48]And about the fourth watch of the night, he came *to where they had returned to land* distressed by rowing, and *told them a parable*, "The Rule of God is like a man whose friends are rowing against the wind, who comes to them walking on the water, wanting to get them past their distress [50]. . . and terror. At once he says, 'Cheer up! Let go of your fear!' [51]And he gets into their boat *and listens to their troubles and*

shares his own, and the wind ceases." But the disciples were completely mystified *by the parable*, [52]for they still did not understand about bread *in the Rule of God*. . . .

45-47 *Ibid.* [48]And he saw that they were distressed in rowing, for the wind was against them. And about the fourth watch of the night he came to them, walking on the sea. He meant to pass them by, [49]but when they saw him walking on the sea they thought it was a ghost, and cried out; [50]for they all saw him, and were terrified. But immediately he spoke to them and said, "Take heart, it is I; have no fear." [51]And he got into the boat with them and the wind ceased. And they were utterly astounded, [52]for they did not understand about the loaves, but their hearts were hardened.

Notes: This parable tells how serenity replaces distress when recovering people talk to one another about their troubles. Popular tradition had long since turned the parable into a story of walking on water, and that is the form in which Mark cast it for his Christian audience. Markôs people knew better. **Walking on water** symbolizes peacefulness in upsetting situations. **Get them past their distress** translates *parerchomai*, an ambiguous verb meaning either "pass by" in the sense of avoiding having to experience something, or "get past" in the sense of getting through something, getting something behind one or over with. Translators have always overlooked the ambiguity while pointing out that "meant to pass them by" in RSV and other versions makes little sense. Later, the dual meanings of *parerchomai* will be crucial to an understanding of its use in the Gethsemane story (14.35). **Listens to their troubles and shares his own** is motivated by **bread** (**loaves** in RSV) in verse 52. To Christian ears an oddity, the reference to **loaves** signaled to the Markôs people that this parable involved the same kind of feeding described in the preceding parable of the loaves and fish, feeding that occurs in their recovery fellowship, caring and sharing in group meetings and one-on-ones. The point is not that the disciples' "hearts were hardened" (RSV, omitted from Sobriety Mark), but that they did not understand the spiritual dynamic exemplified by the parable.

By now Mark has begun to use the disciples in two ways, as surrogates for the Jewish religious officials with whom Jesus argued incessantly, and also as foreshadows of the emergent Christian clergy in his own day. Mark's depictions of Jesus' efforts to make the seemingly dimwitted disciples understand how bread is multiplied in meetings and how feeding leads to serenity actually reflect Jesus' angry disputes with Jewish leaders about their religious practices and the Messianic nature of the Rule of God. At the same time, this portrait of the disciples looks ahead to the Jewish-Christian clergy of Mark's own day, who are wholly oblivious of the recovery spirituality central to Markôs thinking and would be appalled at the anarchy characteristic of Markôs polity.

Omitted Material (6.53-7.23)

The material in 6.53-56 showing people frenziedly coming to Jesus for healings, and the sayings in 7.1-23, serve mainly as an interlude separating the two tellings of the parable of the loaves. Additionally, the picture of the healings acts as camouflage to reassure Christian readers that Jesus was as much a worker of miraculous physical cures as a teacher of spiritual healing. The sayings, in turn, contain reformist but "safe" ideas likely to have been acceptable to both of Mark's audiences, and may have been invented by him for the occasion.

Meeting and Feeding Reprised (8.1-9)

8 [1]In those days, when again a great crowd had gathered and they had nothing to eat, he called his disciples to him and said to them, [2]"I have compassion on the crowd, because they have been with me now three days, and have nothing to eat; [3]and if I send them away hungry to their homes, they will faint on the way; and some of them have come a long way." [4]And his disciples answered him, "How can one feed these men with bread here in the desert?" [5]And he answered *in a parable*, "The Rule of God is like a man who has a fullness of bread to feed the people. [6]And he tells them to recline on the ground, and he takes the words of recovery like seven loaves of bread, and he prays in gratitude, and speaks the wisdom of recovery to them all. [7] . . . [8]*And the people multiply the bread in their comments*, and they all eat and are satisfied, and they take away sevenfold." [9] . . . .

1-4 *Ibid.* [5]And he asked them, "How many loaves have you?" They said, "Seven." [6]And he commanded the crowd to sit down on the ground; and he took the seven loaves, and having given thanks he broke them and gave them to his disciples to set before the people; and they set them before the crowd. [7]And they had a few small fish; and having blessed them, he commanded that these also should be set before them. [8]And they ate, and were satisfied; and they took up the broken pieces left over, seven baskets full. [9]And there were about four thousand people, [10a]and he sent them away.

Notes: Mark repeats the parable of meeting, feeding, and multiplication so that the two tellings plus the episode of loaf and leaven (8.14-21) will form a three-item sequence pointing up the importance of spiritual feeding in the Rule of God. Simply stated, people get better when they meet together and feed on the words of recovery by listening to the leader then sharing their comments around the group. Historically, bread as Word of God was a stock metaphor among the rabbis, nor is it surprising that the Markôs people should have discovered the spiritual potency of having individuals speak in their meetings. The political realities of his day prevented Mark from being more explicit about multiplication. Yet he knew that readers of Sobriety Mark would correctly understand the stories of the amazing residue of bread. Nor is the importance of multiplied bread lost on members of Twelve-Step groups today, who frequently say that the comments in meetings are what they gain most from, what keeps them coming back.

No Miraculous Signs (8.10b-13)

[10b]And immediately he got into the boat with his disciples, and went to the district of Dalmanutha. [11]The Pharisees came and began to argue with him, seeking from him a sign from heaven, to test him. [12]And he sighed deeply in his spirit, and said, "Why does this generation seek a sign? Truly, I say to you, no sign shall be given to this generation." [13]And he left them, and getting into the boat again he departed to the other side.

10b-13 *Ibid.*

Notes: Here Mark uses material from the Sayings Gospel Q (later, Mt 12.31 and Lk 11.29) as an interlude between the second and third parables of feeding. A **sign from heaven** would be a portent perceptible to the senses, extraordinary but not necessarily miraculous. Interpreted as a supernatural increase of a material substance, the feeding of the multitude would constitute just such a sign; yet Jesus says that **no sign shall be given**. Mark's point is that the feedings are to be taken parabolically, not literally.

Bad Leaven (8.14-21)

[14]Once again it had escaped the disciples how to take bread *and multiply it,* although they had a loaf with them in the boat. [15]And he charged them *in a parable*, saying, "Take heed, beware of the leaven of the Pharisees and Herod." [16]And they discussed it with one another, saying, "We have no bread." [17]And being aware of it, Jesus said to them, "Why are you saying that you have no bread? Do you not yet perceive or understand? Are your hearts hardened? [18]Having eyes do you not see, and having ears do you not hear? [19]When I broke the five loaves for the five thousand, how many baskets full of broken pieces did you take up?" They said to him, "Twelve." [20]"And the seven for the four thousand, how many baskets full of broken pieces did you take up?" And they said to him, "Seven." [21]And he said to them, "Do you not yet understand?"

---

[14]Now they had forgotten to bring bread; and they had only one loaf with them in the boat. 15-21 *Ibid.*

Notes: The third feeding parable contains the strongest indictment yet of the disciples' failure to understand how the wisdom of recovery is multiplied. **Escape again** is the root meaning of *epilanthanomai*, usually translated "forget." **Take**, *lambanō*, has multiple meanings; its sense here, as in the other feeding parables (6.41 and 8.6), is grasp and use, not bring with. The idea of verse 14, consistent with the entire passage, is that the disciples still do not understand how to multiply bread. **Bread**, of course, represents words spoken in group meetings. **One loaf in the boat** suggests that the disciples do know that bread is word, and that their duty is to preach it. In Rabbinical thinking, **leaven** was a symbol for whatever corrupts or spoils. In that light, **the leaven of the**

Pharisees and of Herod would refer to preaching that is spirituality corrupt, specifically, that moralizes (**leaven of the Pharisees**) or that commands political obedience (**leaven of Herod**). So in essence Jesus is telling the disciples, "If you still don't see that the way to multiply the word is to allow everyone to have a say, the least you can do is avoid harping on morality and obedience in your own preaching." Jesus then tries to focus the disciples on the amazing residue (**how many baskets full?**) in the episodes of feeding, hoping that they might yet get the point about multiplication. But to no avail.

Actually, the targets of the three feeding parables were not the disciples at all—they knew perfectly well how feeding worked and how the words of recovery were multiplied in their Markôs meetings—but officials of the Jewish synagogues. In his rising mental drunkenness, Jesus had set the spirituality of the Rule of God against that of the synagogue. He had said to the rabbis, in effect, "You're doing it wrong. The Rule of God is more effective spiritually than religious ritual. Stop preaching at people and start multiplying the word the way we do." The polemic in the feeding parables is not as bellicose as that of the vineyard parable that Jesus tells in Jerusalem, but its implicit judgmentalness and combativeness are clear symptoms of his waning sobriety.

Why does Mark cloak the meaning of leaven? The answer is that the emergent Jewish-Christian clergy in 68 A.D., Mark's primary audience, undoubtedly will be required by postwar Roman governors to use dictatorial and moralistic preaching as an instrument for maintaining social order, hence would reject as inauthentic any report that Jesus had opposed the practice.

Stage-One/Stage-Two Healings (7.24-37; 8.22-26)

Canaanite Woman: [24]And from there he arose and went away to the region of Tyre and Sidon. And he entered a house, and would not have had anyone know it; yet he could not be hid. [25]But immediately a woman, whose daughter was suffering a mental disorder, heard of him and came and fell down at his feet. [26]Now the woman was a Greek, a Syrophoenician by birth. And she begged him to heal her daughter. [27]And he said to her, "Let the children first be fed, for it is not right to take the children's bread and throw it to the dogs." [28]But she answered him, "Yes,

Lord; yet even the dogs under the table eat the children's crumbs." [29]And he said to her, "For this saying you may go your way; your daughter has been healed." [30]And she went home, and found the child lying in bed, cured of her disorder.

Deaf-mute: [31]Then he returnd from the region of Tyre, and went through Sidon to the Sea of Galilee, through the region of the Decapolis. [32]And they brought to him a man who was deaf and had an impediment in his speech; and they besought him to lay his hand upon him. [33]And taking him aside from the multitude privately, he put his fingers into his ears, and he spat and touched his tongue; [34]and looking up to heaven, he sighed, and said to him, "Ephphatha," that is, "Be opened." [35]And his ears were opened. Next his tongue was released, and he spoke plainly.

Blind Man: [8.22]And they came to Bethsaida. And some people brought to him a blind man, and begged him to touch him. [23]And he took the blind man by the hand, and led him out of the village; and when he had spit on his eyes and laid his hands upon him, he asked him, "Do you see anything?" [24]And he looked up and said, "I see men, but they look like trees walking." [25]Then again he laid his hands upon his eyes; and he looked intently and was restored and saw everything clearly. [26]And he sent him away to his home, saying, "Do not even enter the village."

7.24-35 *Ibid.* [36]And he charged them to tell no one; but the more he charged them, the more zealously they proclaimed it. [37]And they were astonished beyond measure, saying, "He has done all things well; he even makes the deaf hear and the dumb speak." 8.22-26 *Ibid.*

Notes: These three healing stories are either folklore or Markan fiction. Either way, their function in Christian Mark is camouflage, whereas in Sobriety Mark it is semiotic. The three healings join with the three feeding stories to form a chiasmus (reverse ordering):

1st feeding	1st & 2nd healings	2nd & 3rd feedings	3rd healing
1	2	2	1

The chiasmus is a camouflage that balances healing and feeding in order to divert Christian readers from the scrutiny they might otherwise have given the feeding stories had the latter been presented separately, a scrutiny that might have resulted in their recognizing the parabolic Markôs spirituality involved in the feedings. The folkloric content of the healings further distracts the unsuspecting reader. The story of the woman and daughter involves healing at a distance, which can only be magical. And to first-century sophisticates just as to modern readers, the fingers in the ears and spittle on the tongue and in the eyes, together with the blind man's risible report of men looking like walking trees, identify these stories as folktales without foundation in actuality. Mark's purpose here is to get his Christian readers thinking magically in order to keep their understanding of the multiplication of bread on that plane as well.

In Sobriety Mark, by contrast, the three healing stories serve a semiotic (meaning bearing) function highlighting the stage-one/stage-two motif in the gospel as a whole. All three stories involve a healing effected in two stages: the Canaanite woman procures her daughter's cure after her second entreaty; the deaf-mute receives his speech after his deafness and then his muteness are cured; and the blind man receives full sight after a second laying on of hands. None of this two-stageness belongs to the folkloric aspects of the stories. Markôs people knew that recovery works in two stages: victory over wine, followed by victory over self. Just as Jesus' story played out in two stages, so too the gospel narrative: Galilee then Jerusalem. The hinge between stages one and two of the gospel is Jesus' decision at Caesarea Philippi to go to Jerusalem, and it is immediately before that point (8.27) that Mark concludes the three-item healing sequence. In short, Mark is saying that Jesus' story will now turn from its initial to its final stage.

To Jerusalem (8.27-33)

[27]And Jesus went on with his disciples, to the villages of Caesarea Philippi; and on the way he asked his disciples, "Who do men say that I am?" [28]And they told him, "John the Baptist; and others say Elijah; and others one of the prophets." [29]And he asked them, "But who do you say that I am?" Peter answered him, "You are the Messiah," [30]whereupon, vexed *by Peter's wrong answer*, he charged them not to repeat *that erroneous thinking* to anyone. [31]And

he began to teach them that it behooved himself and them, as persons feeling deeply *about the Rule of God, to proclaim its Messianic status to the Jerusalem* elders, chief priests, and scribes, and be rejected, but then die *to self* and soon thereafter be *spiritually* resurrected. [32]And he said this plainly. And Peter took him, and began to rebuke him. [33]But turning and eyeing his disciples, he rebuked Peter, and said, "Get you into my past, *you're history with me*, just another adversary, because you're not thinking like *someone in the Rule of* God but like *an outsider!*"

27-29 *Ibid.* [30]And he charged them to tell no one about him. [31]And he began to teach them that the Son of Man must suffer many things, and be rejected by the elders and the chief priests and the scribes, and be killed, and after three days rise again. [32]And he said this plainly. And Peter took him, and began to rebuke him. [33]But turning and seeing his disciples, he rebuked Peter, and said, "Get behind me Satan! For you are not on the side of God, but of men."

Notes: In this pivotal scene Jesus disavows Peter's misguided identification of him as Messiah, but then, impelled by the messianism into which his mental drunkenness has coalesced, announces that they must go to Jerusalem to proclaim the Messianic status of the Rule of God and experience self-immolation and spiritual awakening. When Peter tries to dissuade Jesus from these actions, which he presumably considers madness, Jesus rejects him and, by implication, the other disciples. In so doing, ironically, he makes of himself a fanatical solo Messiah, the very thing he knows he is not.

Not to repeat that erroneous thinking: in "tell no one about him" (RSV), *peri auto* is ambiguous, translatable "about him" or "about it." Hence the remark may be contextualized two ways: for Christian Mark, "You and I know that I am the Messiah, but for now we must keep it a secret from the people, so tell no one about it;" for Sobriety Mark, "You may think I am the Messiah but I consider the idea misguided, since the anonymity concept teaches us to place principles before personalities, so do not tell it to anyone." The gist of the first version is, keep it under your hat; of the second, don't spread that nonsense around. Here and in Jesus' three remaining remarks about his possible identity as Messiah (13.21, 13.26, and 14.62), Mark uses ambiguity to satisfy the expectations of both audiences: Christians who believed Jesus had claimed to be the Messiah, and Markôs people who knew that Jesus had assigned Messiah status to their recovery program but never to himself.

Himself and them: *ton huion ton anthropou*, son of man, reflects a Hebrew/Aramaic idiom denoting indefinite or ambiguous reference. *Mark as Recovery Story* reviews scholarship on the term, which a speaker could use to speak in a general way about himself and his associates.[6] Here, Jesus' "son of man" signifies "I and my followers." **Feeling deeply** translates *polla pathein*, universally rendered "suffer much" in order to make the clause a prediction of suffering, but an unusual way to express "suffer" in Greek. *Polla pathein* means to feel much, that is, widely or deeply. Jesus is saying that they should feel strongly enough about the Rule of God to go to Jerusalem and put themselves on the line to proclaim it to the chief religious officials. **Elders and chief priests** establishes Jerusalem as the referent of Jesus' statement.

Die to self/spiritually resurrected: Jesus explains these terms in his upcoming sermon on ego death (8.34-38). **Soon thereafter**: *treis hēmeras*, three days, transliterates a Hebrew idiom meaning in a little while or soon. **Eyeing his disciples**: what Jesus says applies to the other disciples as much as to Peter. **Get you into my past**: the Greek is ambiguous and can also mean depart from me or get back into my following. Markôs people knew that Jesus was rejecting Peter, hence the idiomatic gloss, **you're history with me**. **Just another adversary**: Hebrew "satan," here transliterated into Greek, means adversary and can be so understood, as a generic common noun. **Thinking**: *phronēo*, to think a certain way. **Outsider**: presumably what Peter was arguing against was the idea of ego death, something shunned by unsurrendered addicts outside the Rule of God and those inside who have yet to internalize the Twelve precepts of sobriety. Surprise at Peter's flawed sobriety triggers a second act of mental drunkenness on Jesus' part, the rash decision to reject his followers and go it alone in Jerusalem. The disciples accompany Jesus to Judea, but never again are they coequal message bearers. Jesus in his messianism has made himself terminally unique.

Sermon on Ego Death (8.34-9.1)

[34]And calling the crowd in addition to his Markôs followers, he said, "If anyone wishes to emulate me, he should renounce auto-*empowerment*, voluntarily cooperate in the crucifixion *of self*, and work a spiritual program as I

do. [35]For whoever wishes to preserve his self will lose his life, but whoever lets go of self because of *hearing* me and the wellness message will save his life. [36]For what does it profit anyone to gain the whole world and forfeit his life, [37]since what can anyone pay in exchange for his life? [38]And whoever is scared off by *my being a drunkard* or by my message *of ego death* in a moment of conflictedness or error, so will the messenger of recovery be put off by that person when he comes in the glorious *sobriety* of the Father, *the Higher Power,* along with other dedicated messengers.

9 [1]I nonetheless assure you that there are some standing here who will not taste death before they have experienced empowerment in the Rule of God."

---

[34]And he called to him the multitude with his disciples, and said to them, "If any man would come after me, let him deny himself and take up his cross and follow me. [35]For whoever would save his life will lose it; and whoever loses his life for my sake and the gospel's will save it. [36]For what does it profit a man, to gain the whole world, and forfeit his life? [37]For what can a man give in return for his life? [38]For whoever is ashamed of me and of my words in this adulterous and sinful generation, of him will the Son of man also be ashamed, when he comes in the glory of his Father with the holy angels." [9.1]And he said to them, "Truly, I say to you, there are some standing here who will not taste death before they see the kingdom of God come with power."

Notes: **Calling the crowd**: *proskaleō*, "call aside," is a verb that usually signals teaching delivered to Markôs people. Here, however, instead of addressing only his followers, Jesus delivers his sermon on ego death to the crowd as well. **Auto-empowerment**: **power** in 9.1 retroactively identifies the theme of the sermon as empowerment in the Rule of God, and verses 35-37 identify **self** and self-will as the enemy of such empowerment. Markôs people knew that Jesus was speaking about the central issue of recovery spirituality, power and its source, the self or a Power greater than self. Alcoholics today recognize self-empowerment as the chief opponent of wellness, and failure to renounce it via a Step Three surrender as the surest way to return to drinking. Hence "empower" fills the ellipsis in the verse and together with the reflexive *heauton* yields, "renounce empowering himself." "Auto" then replaces the reflexive himself, and "auto-empowerment" renders the idea in the form of a genderless abstract noun.

Cooperate in the crucifixion of self: Romans often forced crucifixion victims to carry their crossbar to the place of execution. Unsurrendered persons could refuse, an action that presumably led to execution on the spot. Jesus uses this expression, literally, "to take up his cross," to indicate that instead of defiance, persons must cooperate with God in executing, or getting rid of, self. **Work a spiritual program**: *akoloutheō*, follow, would refer to living a spiritual life based on the twelve precepts of sobriety formulated by Jesus. **Self/life**: *psuchē*, used repeatedly in verses 35-37, can mean natural (physical) life, the ego self, mind, or soul. Jesus' point is straightforward: addicts who refuse to die to self generally die physically, either from drink or from the agonistic behavior that drink promotes, whereas those who **let go of self** (surrender, admit powerlessness, ask for help) generally escape untimely physical death.

Because of hearing me: "hearing" fills another ellipsis. Jesus knew that addicted persons do not let go of self "for my sake" (RSV), that is, in a gesture of devotion or allegiance to him as a person, but because of **hearing** the wellness message that he and all other recovering people carry. **In a moment**: *genea*, ordinarily translated generation, means a begetting or a becoming; what is begotten here is inner conflict or flawed thinking at the moment of hearing the message. **Scared off**, *epaischunomai*, ashamed or frightened, expresses colloquially what happens when persons are put off by being approached by an addict (**my being a drunkard**) and/or by the **message of ego death**, whether because they are **conflicted** ("adulterated," that is, impure in their desire for sobriety) or **otherwise err** in their thinking ("sinful" in RSV, *hamartia*, literally a missing of the mark, hence an error). Jesus is not castigating the crowd for moral failures, rather he is telling them that if they are put off by or ashamed of the messenger of recovery, then the messenger will be put off by them and will move on to others who are ready to accept the message. As A.A.s say today, recovery is for those who want it, not for those who need it.

Some standing here: finally, to end the sermon on a positive note, Jesus assures his hearers that some of them *will* get the message, *will* experience the blessing of empowerment in the Rule of God.

PART III: MESSIANISM

At Caesarea Philippi, Jesus becomes disturbed when his followers call him Messiah in violation of his teaching about anonymity and the priority of principles over personalities. He announces that he and they must go to Jerusalem to proclaim the Messianic status not of himself but of the Rule of God, thereby dying to self and rising spiritually as witnesses to stage two of recovery. When Peter and the others protest this course as rash and dangerous, Jesus rejects them and prepares to go it alone, caught up in an obsession that compels him, ironically, to play the role of Messiah, the very role he knows he should not play. His mental drunkenness has turned to overt messianism, a delusional state characterized by the belief that one is uniquely called to save and/or govern others.

Moreover, in shifting his attention from demoniacs, that is, inebriates, to the populace at large, Jesus bypasses stage one of recovery, powerlessness over alcohol, and begins proselytizing the people and their leaders in terms of stage two, powerlessness over self. He turns, in effect, from recovery to religion. Overwhelmed by his messianism, Jesus forgets that defeat by addiction is the unwaivable precondition of wellness in the Rule of God. His sermon on ego death ignores the fact that efforts to achieve self-immolation without prior humiliation by drink lead only to the kind of well-meant religiosity wherein unsurrendered persons futilely try to conquer self by means of self. Not until the Last Supper will Jesus rediscover the truths that powerlessness over drink must precede the surrender of self, and that drinking is a prerequisite to powerlessness, truths he conveys in his words over the Passover cup.

Meanwhile, the story of Jesus' career from Caesarea Philippi to Jerusalem (9.2-10.52) alternates between valid Markôs teaching (Elijah lore, cup of water, stumbling blocks to sobriety, service not rank) and acts of messianic insanity (a feigned healing, guru behavior, acceptance of a Messianic title). By the time he reaches the Holy City, Jesus is drinking again.

Omitted Material (9.2-10)

The transfiguration scene is a fiction invented for Christian Mark. It is not a part of Sobriety Mark. In reprising the baptismal theophany (1.10-11) and resurrection prediction (8.31), it served to reassure Christian readers that despite Jesus' remarks about shame and loss of life (8.34-38) he really was the divine Son of God, who expected worship but nothing as radically humiliating as carrying crosses or dying to self.

Elijah Lore (9.11-13)

[11]And they asked him, "Why do the scribes say that first Elijah must come?" [12]And he said to them, "Elijah comes first to restore all *Passover cups to undrunk fullness*. How does *Isaiah* write of the drinker? Is it not that first he must suffer much and be counted as nothing? [13]But I assure you, Elijah does come . . . ."

---

11 *Ibid.* [12]And he said to them, "Elijah does come first to restore all things; and how is it written of the Son of man, that he should suffer many things and be treated with contempt? [13]But I tell you that Elijah has come, and they did to him whatever they pleased, as it is written of him."

Notes: At the conclusion of the transfiguration scene, Jesus announces that Elijah has come. Christian commentary has focused on the idea of Elijah "coming" in the person of either John the Baptist or Jesus. Markôs lore about Elijah, however, centered around the Elijah cup at Passover and his coming on that occasion. Apparently the Markans looked upon Elijah as a fellow water drinker (I Kgs 17.4 and 10, 18.33-35, 19.5-8) spiritually present to all who renounce Passover wine for water. The origin of the four-cup drinking ritual at Passover, first mentioned in the post-exilic Book of Jubilees, is obscure, as is the traditional obligation to drink the four cups entire. As former wine addicts, Markôs people undoubtedly declined Passover wine just as they did wine at other times. Discussing the reference to Elijah in connection with Jesus' second refusal of drink in the Crucifixion scene (15.35-37), *Mark As Recovery Story* explains the Markan view of Elijah as follows:

> Now Elijah's return was expected as a sign of the Messiah (Mal 4.5-6), and Mark's Jesus announces at the Transfiguration that Elijah has indeed come (9.13). The Crucifixion occurs at Pass-

> over, and part of the Passover wine ritual was—and is—to set a cup for Elijah that remains undrunk. The theory proposed here is that over the years Mark's alcoholics, focused on the eschatological significance of "drinking no more" (14.25) coupled with their image of Elijah as a water drinker, had perpetuated a coterie interpretation of the undrunk Elijah cup as a sign not that Elijah has yet to appear but rather that Elijah *has* come but drinks no wine. In other words, they understood the undrunk Passover cup as a veiled sign of the Age of Messiah, a sign whose recognition depends on a metanoetic reversal of conventional thinking regarding drink, namely, that the joy of wine stems not from consuming it but from deciding to leave it undrunk. (78)

For Markôs people, Elijah comes as a harbinger of Messiah each time a Jew at Passover or a Christian at Eucharist, like Jesus, recognizes wine as the cause of their troubles (14.24), confesses powerlessness and a desire to stop drinking (14.36), and embraces the Messianic Rule of God. Until then, persons must drink. At the Supper, Jesus will offer the cup to his followers (14.23), then voice his belief that the purpose of ritual wine is to quicken the latent alcoholism of all drinkers, thereby enabling the many (*polus*, 14.24)—in effect, everyone—to satisfy the drinking requirement necessary for recognition of illness and entry into recovery. Hence the replaced ellipsis, **to restore all Passover cups to undrunk fullness**. When all Passover and Eucharistic wine remains undrunk, and all former drinkers have found their way into the Rule of God, Messiah will have come indeed.

First Elijah must come refers to the new thinking a Passover drinker experiences when he grasps the truth about Elijah discussed above, namely, that a full cup does not signify Elijah's absence but rather his decision not to drink. **How does Isaiah write**: Jesus is thinking of the Servant Poem of Second Isaiah (52.13-53.12). **Of the drinker**: the Greek "son of man" here refers collectively to Jesus and other drinkers. **First he must suffer much and be counted as nothing**: Markans understood the Servant Poem to say that, for the Servant and for all other addicts, suffering and degradation precede recovery.[7] **Elijah does come**: Jesus assures his followers that recovery does occur after the necessary suffering. The remainder of verse 13 in the RSV appears to be an addition by a hand other than Mark's.

Mark's use of the Elijah figure in the crucifixion scene (15.35-37) also involves Elijah's reputation as a nondrinker and is discussed in the notes on that passage.

A Cup of Water (9.38-41)

[38]John said to him, "Teacher, we saw a man curing drunkards in your name, and we forbade him, because he was not following us." [39]But Jesus said, "Do not forbid him; for no one who invokes empowerment by calling 'God, help!' is going to turn around and speak evil of me. [40]For he that is not against us is with us. [41]For truly, I say to you, whoever gives a person a cup of water to drink so that they might know the meaning of Messiah will by no means lose his reward, *the joy of service*."

---

[38]John said to him, "Teacher, we saw a man casting out demons in your name, and we forbade him, because he was not following us." [39]But Jesus said, "Do not forbid him; for no one who does a mighty work in my name will be able soon after to speak evil of me. [40]For he that is not against us is with us. [41]For truly, I say to you, whoever gives you a cup of water to drink because you bear the name of Christ, will by no means lose his reward."

Notes: **A cup of water to drink** was the entrance rite for newcomers to the Markôs program, initiating them into the Messianic Rule of God. Members knew that Elijah had begun his ministry by requesting from the widow of Zarephath a cup of water and a piece of bread (I Kgs 17.10-11). They viewed bread as a symbol of the wisdom of recovery, and water as a counter-symbol to wine, one's drink in sobriety. Because this initiatory rite was anathematized by Christian wine drinkers (Heb 10.29, for example, promises severe punishment for any who "deem unclean the blood of the covenant," that is, who refuse to drink Eucharistic wine), Mark could not mention it in connection with Jesus' baptism and early work with drunkards, where it first came into play, but concealed it deep in his book, encoded in a non sequitur to verses 38-40 that Christians would interpret as merely a passing illustration of Jesus' kindness and charity. **God, help!**: the name "Jesus" consists of the roots God and help or save, which convey its meaning here. Neither Hebrew nor Aramaic had a word for "meaning," and both used the expression "in the name of" to signify the meaning associated with a particular name. The same principle motivates the translation of *en onomati . . . christou* as **the meaning of Messiah**, which is metanoia in the Rule of God, the certain consequence of renouncing wine for water at the appointed time. In verse 39, **no one . . . is going to . . . speak evil**

of me reflects the Markans' experience, ratified by that of A.A.s today, that no matter how angry addicts might be initially, their rancor changes to gratitude when their plea for help is answered by empowerment. Persons who call on God for help in crises do not themselves "do a mighty work" (*poiēsei dunamin*) but rather **invoke empowerment** from a higher power; the distinction is crucial to Markôs spirituality. Finally, the **reward** of giving the cup of water can only be **the joy of service**, the privilege of carrying the message of recovery to those who still suffer.

Feigned Healing (9.14-29)

[14]And when they came to the disciples, they saw a great crowd about them, and scribes arguing with them. [15]And immediately all the crowd, when they saw him, were greatly amazed, and ran up to him and greeted him. [16]And he asked them, "What are you discussing with them?" [17]And one of the crowd answered him, "Teacher, I brought my son to you, for he has a dumb spirit; [18]and whenever it seizes him, it dashes him down; and he foams and grinds his teeth and becomes rigid; and I asked your disciples to cast it out, and they were not able." [19]And he answered them, "O faithless generation, how long am I to bear with you? Bring him to me." [20]And they brought the boy to him; and when the spirit saw him, immediately it convulsed the boy, and he fell on the ground and rolled about, foaming at the mouth. [21]And Jesus asked his father, "How long has he had this?" And he said, "From childhood. [22]And it has often cast him into the fire and into the water, to destroy him; but if you can do anything, have pity on us and help us." [23]And Jesus said to him, "If you can! All things are possible to him who believes." [24]Immediately the father of the child cried out and said, "I believe; help my unbelief!" [25]And when Jesus saw that a crowd came running together, he rebuked the unclean spirit, saying to it, "You dumb and deaf spirit, I command you, come out of him, and never enter him again." [26]And after crying out and convulsing him terribly, it came out, and the boy was like a corpse; so that most of them said,

"He is dead." [27]But Jesus took him by the hand and lifted him up, and he arose.

14-27, *Ibid.* [28]And when he had entered the house, his disciples asked him privately, "Why could we not cast it out?" [29]And he said to them, "This kind cannot be driven out by anything but prayer."

Notes: Former drunkards often tell anecdotes about their alcoholic craziness to celebrate the fact that they no longer act so outrageously. In his recovery story after his return to Galilee, Jesus must have enjoyed recounting the present incident. In the grips of unbridled messianism en route to Jerusalem, he had pretended to heal an epileptic boy who had only gone into, then come out of, a routine seizure. Though its physiology was unknown, epilepsy (from *epilēpsia*, "seizure") was familiar to first-century doctors as an illness unrelated to demon possession. Mark's specific description, **dashes him down; and he foams and grinds his teeth and becomes rigid**, is obviously meant to denote seizure disorder, a sickness the boy had had **from childhood**. Mark believed that Christians would interpret the story as an exorcism and/or healing, whereas Markôs readers would only smile wryly at the memory of Jesus' ridiculous behavior.

O faithless generation, how long am I to bear with you? is the remark of a self-indulgently exasperated guru, not of a humbled recovering person. Verses 28-29 are post-Markan.

Rejoining Humanity (9.30-32; 10.32-34)

[9.30]They went on from there and passed through Galilee. And he would not have anyone know it; [31]for he was teaching his disciples, saying to them, "The man will be rejoined to men . . . ." [32]But they did not understand the saying, and they were afraid to ask him.

[10.32]And they were on the road, going up to Jerusalem, and Jesus was walking ahead of them; and they were agitated, and those who followed were afraid. And referring again to the Twelve *sobriety precepts*, he began to tell them what was to happen to him, [33]saying, "Behold, we are going up to Jerusalem; and the man will be rejoined to humanity . . . ."

[9.30]They went on from there and passed through Galilee. And he would not have anyone know it; [31]for he was teaching his disciples, saying to them, "The Son of man will be delivered into the hands of men, and they will kill him; and when he is killed, after three days he will rise." [32]But they did not understand the saying, and they were afraid to ask him.

[10.32]And they were on the road, going up to Jerusalem, and Jesus was walking ahead of them; and they were amazed, and those who followed were afraid. And taking the Twelve again, he began to tell them what was to happen to him, [33]saying, "Behold, we are going up to Jerusalem; and the Son of man will be delivered to the chief priests and the scribes, and they will condemn him to death, and deliver him to the Gentiles; [34]and they will mock him, and spit upon him, and scourge him, and kill him; and after three days he will rise."

Notes: **Would not have anyone know it** indicates that insider lore is involved in the understanding of what Christians traditionally call the passion predictions. **Agitated and . . . afraid**: presumably these emotions were triggered by the sight of Jesus' willful messianism en route to Jerusalem. **Referring again to the Twelve sobriety precepts** suggests that one or more of the Twelve concerned the process of spiritual growth to which the saying "man rejoined to men" pertained. **Man rejoined to men**: in recovering from the ravages of drink, a process that involves admitting wrongs and amending one's conduct, addicts learn how radically separated from other people their illness had made them. They often say, "I feel I've rejoined the human race" or "become a human being again." The Aramaic phrase "man rejoined to men" or "person rejoined to persons" was the first-century equivalent of this cliché. Its ambiguity should be obvious. To Christian readers it referred to Jesus' betrayal and arrest by the authorities, hence the usual translation of *paradidōmi* as "deliver" or "hand over" in the sense of betray. But to Markôs people it meant a recovering person getting better and being "given over" into restored membership in the human race. Christians believed that Jesus had predicted his crucifixion and resurrection, whereas Markans knew that what he had voiced was his hope that in Jerusalem he would stop playing God and become a truly human being at last. The narrator's **but they did not understand the saying** refers to Christians' failure to comprehend the saying in its recovery sense. The final clauses of 9.31, as well as the second half of 10.33 and all of 10.34, are additions by Mark or a redactor to reinforce the Christian reading. Realistically they cannot have been spoken by Jesus and are not a part of Sobriety Mark.

Stumbling Blocks (10.13-16, 23-31)

10 [13]And they were bringing children to him, that he might touch them; and the disciples rebuked them. [14]But when Jesus saw it he was displeased, and said to them, "Let the children come to me without hindrance, for it is *the childlike* who get the Rule of God. [15]Truly, I say to you, whoever does not seize the proffered Rule of God with *the whole-hearted zeal* of a child shall not enter it." . . .

[23]And Jesus looked around and said to his disciples, "How hard it will be for those who have riches to enter the Rule of God!" [24]And the disciples were amazed by his words. But Jesus said to them again, "Children, how hard it is for those who trust in riches to enter the Rule of God! [25]It is easier for a camel to go through the eye of a needle than for a rich man to enter the Rule of God." [26]And they were exceedingly astonished, and said to him, "Then who can be saved?" [27]Jesus looked at them and said, "With men it is impossible, but not with God; for all things are possible with God." [28]Peter began to say to him, "Behold, we have left everything and followed you." [29]Jesus said, "Truly, I say to you, there is no one who has left house or brothers or sisters or mother or father or children or lands, because of me and the wellness message, [30]who will not receive a hundredfold now in this time, houses and brothers and sisters and mothers and children and lands, ..."

10.13 *Ibid.* [14]But when Jesus saw it he was displeased, and said to them, "Let the children come to me, do not hinder them; for to such belongs the Rule of God. [15]Truly, I say to you, whoever does not receive the Rule of God like a child shall not enter it." [16]And he took them in his arms and blessed them, laying his hands upon them.

10.23-30a *Ibid.* [30b]". . . with persecutions, and in the age to come eternal life. [31]But many that are first will be last, and the last first."

Notes: Here Jesus identifies three things that prevent addicts from getting the Markôs program (Rule of God): lack of wholeheartedness in reaching out to accept it, trust in material wealth to somehow solve their problem, and reliance upon family members to do the same. Apparently what appealed to Jesus about children was their enthusiastic and unquestioning acceptance of any new thing offered them. **Seize the proffered Rule of God**: *dechomai*, regularly translated "receive," differs from the usual word for receive, *lambanō*, and denotes an enthusaistic acceptance of something offered rather than a one-sided taking, which is the meaning of *lambanō*. **The childlike**: obviously, Jesus is not talking literally about children but about sick adults who must learn to act like children if they are to recover. **Trust in riches**: recovering persons of means regularly say that reliance on their wealth only prolonged their suffering. The same is true of misplaced reliance on the support of family members. **Receive a hundredfold now in this time**: addicts who refuse to put their recovery ahead of possessions and family members usually get worse instead of better and lose both wealth and family, whereas those who do the opposite generally find that they regain possessions and the respect of loved ones, often to a greater degree than before. While Jesus' teaching here reflects the spirit of the Cupmaster fellowship, its tone is that of the guru. A.A. experience shows that alcoholics who play the preacher are setting themselves up for relapse.

Omitted Sayings (9.42-10.12; 10.17-22)

Jesus' conduct en route to Jerusalem alternated between valid Markôs teaching and times when his messianic obsession overwhelmed him. One manifestation of the latter was extremist and absolutist preaching. Mark has included three illustrations: 9.42-50 presents an image of sinners drowning with millstones tied round their necks, cutting off hands and feet, plucking out eyes, and suffering hellfire; 10.1-12 absolutizes the Mosaic teaching on divorce; and 10.17-22 tells wealthy persons that to attain eternal life they must sell off their goods and give the proceeds to the poor. This kind of moral fanaticism sometimes finds favor among religious people, but it has nothing of the Rule of God about it, nothing of live and let live, taking one's own inventory not the other person's, being hard on oneself and easy on others. It is the mark of a messianic caught up in religious extremism, which is what Jesus had become by this point in his career. He is close to resuming drinking.

Servant Not Overlord (9.33-37)

33And they came to Capernaum; and when he was in the house he asked them, "What were you discussing on the way?" [34]But they were silent; for on the way they had discussed with one another who was the greatest. [35]And sitting down he invoked the Twelve *sobriety precepts* and said to them, "If anyone would be of the first *rank spiritually*, he must be last *in authority* and the servant of all." . . .

33-34 *Ibid.* [35]And he sat down and called the Twelve; and he said to them, "If any one would be first, he must be last of all and servant of all." [36]And he took a child, and put him in the midst of them; and taking him in his arms, he said to them, [37]"Whoever receives one such child in my name receives me; and whoever receives me, receives not me but him who sent me."

Notes: Apparently one of the **Twelve sobriety precepts** promised spiritual fulfillment as a result of carrying the message to others. Then as now, service in the Rule of God means the giving of self evangelically, whereas attempts to assume **authority** lead only to spiritual dryness. The strangely disjunct material in verses 36-37 looks like an addition by church officials exploiting the image of the child to deflect criticism of their own assumption of authority.

Jesus Drinks Again (10.35-39)

[35]And James and John, the sons of Zebedee, came forward to him, and said to him, "Teacher, we want you to do for us whatever we ask of you." [36]And he said to them, "What do you want me to do for you?" [37]And they said to him, "Grant us exalted positions equal to the glorious exaltedness in store for you." [38]But Jesus said to them, "You do not know what you are asking. Are you prepared to drink *again* of the cup from which I am drinking, to get caught up *again* in the *wine* dipping which I am caught up in?" [39]And they said to him, "We are." And Jesus said to them, "Then the cup that I am drinking you too will drink, and the dipping that I am caught up in you too will be caught up in."

35-36 *Ibid.* [37]And they said to him, "Grant us to sit, one at your right hand and one at your left, in your glory." [38]But Jesus said to them, "You do not know what you are asking. Are you able to drink the cup that I drink, or to be baptized with the baptism with which I am baptized?" [39]And they said to him, "We are able." And Jesus said to them, "The cup that I drink you will drink; and with the baptism with which I am baptized, you will be baptized."

Notes: Two of the disciples ask Jesus for positions of exalted authority. Despite his messianic behaviors to the contrary, Jesus knows that the only kind of exaltedness sober addicts should seek is spiritual, and that the way to achieve it is through helping others attain sobriety. In correcting the mental drunkenness underlying the disciples' request, however, Jesus discloses the fact that he himself has returned to drink.

Cup: To Christians, "cup" referred to the suffering Jesus would undergo in crucifixion, whereas to Markôs people it signified alcoholic drinking and the pain it causes. **From which I am drinking**: the present tense in Greek equals the English present progressive ("I am drinking") and indicates ongoing action. Jesus is drinking again.

This fact is confirmed in Jesus' subsequent remark about baptism. As discussed earlier, the Greek *baptizō* meant to dip, specifically, to immerse oneself in water for bathing, to wash garments or dye fabric, or (the meaning here and in 1.9-10) to dip a cup of water or wine from a larger vessel. Figuratively, *baptizō* meant to undergo a painful and overwhelming ordeal. Unglossed, the final predicates in verse 38, ordinarily transliterated "be baptized in the baptism in which I am baptized," would read, "be dipped in the dipping in which I am dipped." Here the first and third uses are figurative references to a forced ordeal, the second is a literal reference to dipping drink; hence the translation **caught up in the . . . dipping which I am caught up in. Wine dipping**: in its bibulous sense *baptizō* seems also to have been an item of drinking slang. Just as speakers today say colloquially of a person who has returned to drinking after a period of abstinence, "he's boozing again," Greek speakers said, "he's dipping again." **Get caught up in** renders Jesus' figurative use of *baptizō* to mean overwhelmed by the experience of active addiction. **Again**: the restored ellipsis emphasizes that the issue is one of a return to drinking, of re-addiction.

Then the cup that I am drinking you too will drink: Jesus predicts a similar return by his disciples. He is saying what A.A. oldtimers often say to defiant newcomers: "You need to go out and drink some more; alcohol hasn't broken you yet." Jesus' prediction is fulfilled at the Last Supper, when all of the disciples drink from the Passover cup.

Discourse on Service (10.40-45)

[40]"But it is not my place to grant exaltedness, which is reserved for those for whom it has been prepared." [41]And when the ten heard it, they began to be displeased at James and John. [42]And Jesus called them to him and said to them, "You know that persons thinking to rule the nations lord it over people, and their great ones exercise authority over them. [43]But not so among those of you *in the Rule of God*, for whoever among you would be great *in sobriety* must be the servant of the rest, [44]and whoever would be in the first *rank spiritually* must be the slave of all. [45]For the mission of any recovering person is not to be served but to serve, to devote himself to ransoming many *from the bondage of self*."

---

[40]"But to sit at my right hand or at my left is not mine to grant, but it is for those for whom it has been prepared." [41]And when the ten heard it, they began to be indignant at James and John. [42]And Jesus called them to him and said to them, "You know that those who are supposed to rule over the Gentiles lord it over them, and their great men exercise authority over them. [43]But it shall not be so among you; but whoever would be great among you must be your servant, [44]and whoever would be first among you must be slave of all. [45]For the Son of man also came not to be served but to serve, and to give his life as a ransom for many."

Notes: Even though he has resumed drinking, Jesus' words here reflect sober thinking untainted by his ongoing messianism. **Displeased**: the ten were jealously angry that the two would ask for something they also coveted. Jesus knows that **great** and **first** should pertain not to temporal or religious status but to contented sobriety achieved through service, through carrying the messsage to other sufferers. Attempts to exercise authority and **lord it over people** only undermine sobriety. **Any recovering person**: "son of man" in RSV refers not just to Jesus but to all recovering addicts. **The bondage of self**: the final victory over addiction, stage two of recovery, is freedom from self. Drinkers ultimately learn that their addiction to alcohol was but a symptom, a consequence of their enslavement to the illusion of self-empowerment.

This passage is connected to the Suffering Servant poem in Isaiah 52.13-53.12. **To ransoming many**: Greek *lutron,* "ransom," translates the

Hebrew *'āšām* of Is 53.10, where it is rendered "guilt offering." The verse reads:

> (Is 53.10) Surely it was God who decided to crush him with pain. And yet, if he surrenders his self as a guilt offering, he will see his offspring and lengthen his days, and the plan of God will succeed in his hand.

Apparently Jesus and the Markôs people identified Isaiah's Servant as an ex-drunkard, a former street alcoholic whose suffering and surrender serve as examples inspiring ordinary drinkers, religious and otherwise, to recognize their latent addiction and admit their powerlessness.

Many (*polus*) also links this passage both to the Servant poem and to Jesus' words over the wine at the Last Supper (Mk 14.24). Central to Jesus' message to the wider world on that occasion, once he had sobered up for good, was the idea which he found in Isaiah and expresses here in seminal form: although advanced addicts like the Servant may be few in the populace at large, their recovery experience can benefit many. Isaiah summarizes the Servant's story thus:

> (Is 53.11) In return for the affliction of his soul he shall drink [the wine of sobriety], deeply, until sated. His knowledge of submission [that is, powerlessness] will have vindicated him, and will free the multitudes from bondage.[8]

Playing Messiah (10.46-52)

[46]And they came to Jericho; and as he was leaving Jericho with his disciples and a great multitude, Bartimaeus, a blind beggar, the son of Timaeus, was sittting by the roadside. [47]And when he heard that it was Jesus of Nazareth, he began to cry out and say, "Jesus, Son of David, have mercy on me!" [48]And many rebuked him, telling him to be silent; but he cried out again, "Son of David, have mercy on me!" [49]And Jesus stopped and said, "Call him."

46-49a *Ibid.* [49b]And they called the blind man, saying to him, "Take heart; rise, he is calling you." [50]And throwing off his mantle he sprang up and came to Jesus. [51]And Jesus said to him, "What do you want me to do for you?" And the blind man said to him, "Master, let me receive my sight." [52]And Jesus said to him, "Go your way, your faith has made you well." And immediately he received his sight and followed him on the way.

Notes: Contrary to his teaching about non-self-agrandizing service, the Bartimaeus episode, minus its camouflage as a healing, depicts Jesus' acceptance of the twice-uttered salutation **Son of David**, a Messiah title with political implications. Jesus' imperious **call him** suggests not just that he fails to reject the title but that he publicly embraces it. The stage is set for Jesus' drunken entrance into Jerusalem and rampage in the Temple.

PART IV: RELAPSE

Part four of Sobriety Mark depicts the consequences of Jesus' return to drinking. It begins with chapter eleven, which contains the most elaborate camouflage of the entire gospel. Markôs people knew the real story: Having entered Jerusalem wine drunk, Jesus had gone to the Temple intoxicated and exhorted whoever would listen to renounce wine for water and embrace the Rule of God. Ignored as a crazed drunkard, he had gone berserk and had tried to wrest the drinking vessels from the people, pilgrims and religious minions alike (verse 16). In so doing he caused a near riot upsetting the operations of Temple merchants and resulting in the issuance of a warrant for his arrest. But there was no prearranged procurement of a donkey, no Messianic salutations, no leafy branches or hosannas (verses 2-10), no quarrel with the merchants (verse 15) or preaching to Temple officials (verse 17), and no teaching concerning the blighted figtree (verses 20-25). These are Markan contrivances concealing the scandalous story of Jesus' rampage (verses 15-16).

Riding a donkey The Jerusalem entrance on a donkey (verses 2-10) reflects a Christian misunderstanding of what the Galilean Markôs people had reported, turning on the Aramaic "donkey/ wine" pun. *Mark As Recovery Story* explains this pun as follows:

> In the northern Aramaic dialect spoken by Jesus and the disciples, the words meaning "donkey" and "wine" were pronounced and written exactly the same. The two formed a perfect pun. This fact is confirmed by the Aramaic expert George Lamsa and in a Talmudic anecdote in which Jerusalem merchants ridicule a Galilean who cannot clearly pronounce what he wants to buy, something to ride on (a

> donkey = *hamār*) or something to drink (wine = *hamar*). Thus, what speakers of other dialects and languages would regard as two different statements—in English, "donkeyed" or "on a donkey" versus "wined" or "wine drunk"—sounded the same in Jesus' Galilean Aramaic. Unaware of the ambiguity, Markôs people telling Jesus' story thought they were saying that Jesus entered the city wine drunk, whereas their nonalcoholic compatriots, unprepared to think of Jesus as a drunkard, thought they were hearing that Jesus entered the city on a donkey, and that is how they remembered the story. (211)[9]

Given the Christian understanding of the donkey as a Messianic prophecy fulfillment, it was only natural that Mark would embellish his story with heroic trappings such as the unridden beast (11.2), carpeted path (11.8), and reference to a storied progenitor, here King David (11.10).

Cursing the figtree Verses 12-14 depict a hungry Jesus on his way to the Temple cursing a figtree for barrenness in its off season. The story has long puzzled interpreters. Apparently it reflects an anecdote Jesus told illustrating his drunken condition as evidenced by petulant acting out. Realistically the tree was unaffected by Jesus' imprecation, and the material in verses 20-25 is Markan camouflage meliorating the inanity of Jesus' act.

Violence in the Temple Verses 15-16 depict an act of violence harmful, like all violence, to those upon whom it was visited as well as to its perpetrator. Christians have long excused Jesus' action as "righteous anger." In fact, the merchants in the Temple were performing valuable services for pilgrims and were strictly supervised by Temple police so that they would not, by crooked dealings, provoke a riot and cause the Romans to ban religious assembly. They were not the "thieves" of Jer 7.11. In any case, upsetting the merchants (verse 15) was collateral damage quite unintended by Jesus, whose actual target (verse 16) was persons preparing to engage in religious drinking, whether in the Temple or the upcoming Passover celebration.

The triad Beyond its function as camouflage, this triadic event sequence has parabolic value. The donkey/wine pun indicates Jesus' drunkenness and introduces the theme of intoxication. Cursing the figtree represents simple drunken behavior, an angry but harmless outburst much like swearing at a broken shoelace. If alcohol had no consequences greater than cursed figtrees, most would think it benign. By contrast, the assault in the Temple depicts the harm that results when inebriation catalyzes prior mental drunkenness and triggers violence against persons. Alcoholics know from bitter experience that people who drunkenly act out so-called justified anger undermine their own serenity and cause fighting and trouble all around.

Chapter twelve shows the verbal hostility towards religious officials with which Jesus followed up his attack on drinkers in the Temple. Drunkenly ignoring the fact that he knows he is not the Messiah, that Messiah is not a person, Jesus attacks the authorities for failing to acknowledge his Messiahship. Thereafter, in sally after sally of combative rhetoric, Jesus exposes the sham, hypocrisy, and veniality of the Jerusalem leaders. Yet his argumentative virtuosity changes no minds and produces only a warrant for his arrest. Although his parable of the vineyard (verses 1-12) blatantly portrays the officials as unadmitted addicts, never once does Jesus invite them to acknowledge their illness and come into the Rule of God. Instead he seeks to dominate them, thereby setting the stage for catastrophe.

Temple Rampage (11.1-25)

11 [1]And when they drew near to Jerusalem, to Bethphage and Bethany, at the Mount of Olives, he sent two of his disciples, [2]and said to them, "Go into the village opposite you, and immediately as you enter it you will find a store of wine close kept. Loose it and bring it.". . . [7]And they brought the wine beneath their garments, and he became wine drunk. . . . [12]The next morning, when they left Bethany, he was hungry. [13]And seeing in the distance a figtree in leaf, he went to see if he could find anything on it. When he came to it, he found nothing but leaves, for it was not the season for figs. [14]And he said to it, "May no one ever eat fruit from you again." And his disciples heard it. [15]And they came to Jerusalem. And he entered the Temple and began pushing aside buyers and sellers there, and overturning money-changers' tables and pigeon-sellers' seats, [16]in his attempt to prevent persons from deploying *wine* vessels for use in Temple *rituals*. . . . [18]And the chief priests and the scribes heard *about the ruckus* and sought a way to destroy him, for they feared him *as a public agitator*. . . .

---

[1]And when they drew near to Jerusalem, to Bethphage and Bethany, at the Mount of Olives, he sent two of his disciples, [2]and said to them, "Go into the village opposite you, and immediately as you enter it you will find a colt tied, on which no one has ever sat; untie it and bring it. [3]If any one says to you, 'Why are you doing this?' say, 'The Lord has need of it and will send it back here immediately.'" [4]And they went away, and found a colt tied at the door out in the open street; and they untied it. [5]And those who stood there said to them, "What are you doing, untying the colt?" [6]And they told them what Jesus had said; and they let them go. [7]And they brought the colt to Jesus, and threw their garments on it; and he sat upon it. [8]And many spread their garments on the road, and others spread leafy branches which they had cut from the fields. [9]And those who went before and those who followed cried out, "Hosanna! Blessed is he who comes in the name of the Lord! [10]Blessed is the kingdom of our father David that is coming! Hosanna in the highest!" 12-14 *Ibid*. [15]And they came to Jerusalem. And he entered the Temple and began to drive out those who sold and those who bought in the Temple, and he overturned the tables of the money-changers and the seats of those who sold pigeons. [16]and he would not allow anyone to carry anything through the Temple. [17]And he taught, and said to them, "Is it not written, 'My house shall be called a house of prayer for all the nations'? But you have made it a den of robbers." [18]And the chief priests and the scribes heard it and sought a way to destroy him; for they feared him, because all the multitude was astonished at his teaching.

Notes: Verses 3-6, 8-11, 17, and 19-25 are camouflage in Christian Mark, hence omitted. **A store of wine . . . brought the wine . . . wine drunk**: while it backgrounds the entire passage, the donkey/wine pun specifically underlies verses 2 and 7, the only parts of the story that portray actuality. Mark uses colt, *pōlos*, in verses 2-7 to avoid calling attention to the Aramaic pun and arousing suspicions, but everyone knew the beast was a donkey. **Wine close kept** comes from "a colt [donkey] tied." **Loose it** comes from "untie it." Whose wine it was, what it was intended for, and how Jesus knew about it, are questions that cannot be answered. **Brought the wine beneath their garments** comes from "threw their garments on it [the donkey]." **He became wine drunk** comes from "he sat upon it [the donkey]."

Pushing aside: *ekballein* in verse 15 is generally translated in its exorcism sense, "drive out," on the assumption that Jesus' purpose was to banish commercial activity from the Temple. **Wine vessels**: verse 16 is invariably taken as an extension of the thought in verse 15 with *skeuos* generically translated thing, goods, or merchandise. *Skeuos*, however, means "vessels," ranging from the silver wine vessels long used by the Temple priests to the cups and jugs used by pilgrims for drinking their private ceremonials. **Attempt to prevent**: literally verse 16 says that Jesus "would not allow" (*aphiēmi*, to permit or suffer) the carrying of vessels, but realistically this can only mean that he attempted to prevent it. **Deploying**: "carry" in the Christian version renders *diapherō*, to carry through, and a second *dia* follows *skeuos. Diapherō* can mean carry to and fro, carry around, or simply deploy, and the second *dia* can mean for or with a view to. Hence the reading here. In short, Jesus' objective was not to suppress commercial activity but to quash religious drinking. **Began pushing aside**: verse 15, therefore, merely reports the chaos Jesus caused in violently acting out his anger at people's failure to heed his call.

Jesus' original intention, apparently, was to exhort people to renounce religious drinking in favor of water; and his proclamation in the Temple reported in Jn 7.37, "If anyone thirst, let him come to me and drink [water]," reflects a tirade against wine immediately preceding the berserk attempt to seize worshippers' drinking vessels. Thereafter Jesus enters into hostile verbal conflict with the Jerusalem religious leaders, but it is his drunken efforts to wrest the drinking vessels from people in the Temple that provoke crisis and apocalypse.

Warfare in the Vineyard (12.1-12)

12 [1]And he began to speak to *the religious authorities* in parables. "A man planted a vineyard, and set a hedge around it, and dug a pit for the wine press, and built a tower, and let it out to tenants, and went into another country. [2]When the time came, he sent a servant to the tenants, to get from them some of the fruit of the vineyard. [3]And they took him and beat him, and sent him away empty-handed. [4]And he sent to them another servant, and they wounded him in the head, and treated him shamefully. [5]And he sent another, and him they killed; and so with many others, some they beat and some they killed. [6]He had still one other, a beloved son; finally he sent him to them saying, 'They will respect my son.' [7]But those tenants said to one another, 'This is the heir; come, let us kill him, and the inheritance will be ours.' [8]And they took him and killed him, and cast him out of the vineyard. [9]What will the owner of the vineyard do? He will come and destroy the tenants, and give the vineyard to others.". . . [12]And they tried to arrest him, but feared the multitude, for they perceived that he had told the parable against them; so they left him and went away.

1-9 *Ibid.* [10]"Have you not read the scripture: 'The stone which the builders rejected has become the head of the corner; [11]this is the Lord's doing, and it is marvelous in our eyes'?" 12 *Ibid.*

Notes: Markôs people would have viewed the "wild grapes" of the Isaian vineyard (5.1-6) as a symbol of alcoholism. Angered by his rejection, Jesus declares verbal war on the chief priests and scribes and elders and reshapes the Isaian material into an attack parable in which the owner represents God and the tenants the authorities. Their refusal to give the owner his share means that they intend to drink all the wine themselves. They are alcoholics. So far so good. But in casting himself as the owner's son, Jesus plays Messiah when he knows that Messiahship lies in principles not persons. He accuses and threatens when he should be offering recovery and telling about his own addiction. He slams the authorities for disobedience to God when he should be exhorting them to admit their powerlessness over alcohol. In his bellicose drunkenness, Jesus makes a mockery of Markan procedures for carrying the message to suffering addicts. He has all but reached his nadir.

Rhetorical Combat (11.27-33; 12.13-44)

Sham authority: [27]And they came again to Jerusalem. And as he was walking in the Temple, the chief priests and the scribes and the elders came to him, [28]and they said to him, "By what authority are you doing these things, or who gave you authority to do them?" [29]Jesus said to them, "I will ask you a question; answer me, and I will tell you by what authority I do these things. [30]Was the baptism of John from heaven or from men? Answer me." [31]And they argued with one another, "If we say, 'From heaven,' he will say, 'Why then did you not believe him?' [32]But shall we say, 'From men'?" - they were afraid of the people, for all held that John was a real prophet. [33]So they answered Jesus, "We do not know." And Jesus said to them, "Neither will I tell you by what authority I do these things."

Temporality: [13]And they sent to him some of the Pharisees and some of the Herodians, to entrap him in his talk. [14]And they came and said to him, "Teacher, we know that you are true, and care for no man; for you do not regard the position of men, but truly teach the way of God. Is it lawful to pay taxes to Caesar, or not? [15]Should we pay them, or should we not?" But knowing their hypocrisy, he said to them, "Why put me to the test? Bring me a coin, and let me look at it." [16]And they brought one. And he said to them, "Whose likeness and inscription is this?" They said to him, "Caesar's." [17]Jesus said to them, "Render to Caesar the things that are Caesar's, and to God the things that are God's." And they were amazed at him.

No privileged knowledge: [18]And the Sadducees came to him, who say that there is no resurrection; and they asked him a question, saying, [19]"Teacher, Moses wrote for us that if a man's brother dies and leaves a wife, but leaves no child, the man must take the wife, and raise up children for his brother. [20]There were seven brothers; the first took a wife, and when he died left no children; [21]and the second took her, and died, leaving no children; and the third likewise; [22]and the seventh left no children. Last of all the woman also died. [23]In the resurrection whose wife will she be? For the seven had her as wife." [24]Jesus said to them, "Is not this why you are wrong, that you know neither the scriptures nor the power of God? [25]For when they rise from the dead, they neither marry nor are given in marriage, but are like the angels in heaven. [26]And as for the dead being raised, have you not read in the book of Moses, in the passage about the bush, how God said to them, 'I am the God of Abraham, and the God of Isaac, and the God of Jacob'? [27]He is not God of the dead, but of the living; you are quite wrong."

Unrenounced offices: [28]And one of the scribes came up and heard them disputing with one another, and seeing that he answered them well, asked him, "Which commandment is the first of all?" [29]Jesus answered, "The first is, 'Hear, O Israel: The Lord our God, the Lord is one; [30]and you shall love the Lord your God with all your heart, and with all your soul, and with all your mind, and with all your strength.' [31]The second is this, 'You shall love your neighbor as yourself.' There is no other commandment greater than these." [32]And the scribe said to him, "You are right, Teacher; you have truly said that he is one, and there is no other but he; [33]and to love him with all the heart, and with all the understanding, and with all the strength, and to love one's neighbor as oneself, is much more than all whole burnt offerings and sacrifices." [34]And when Jesus saw that he answered wisely, he said to him, "You are not far from the Rule of God." And after that no one dared to ask him any question. [35]And as Jesus taught in the Temple, he said, "How can the scribes say that the Christ is the son of David? [36]David himself, inspired by the Holy Spirit, declared, 'The Lord said to my Lord, Sit at my right hand till I put thy enemies under my feet.' [37]David himself calls him Lord; so how is he his son?" And the great throng heard him gladly.

Veniality: [38]And in his teaching he said, "Beware of the scribes, who like to go about in long robes, and to have salutations in the market places [39]and the best seats in the synagogues and the places of honor at feasts, [40]who devour widows' houses and for a pretense make long prayers. They will receive the greater condemnation."

Unrelinquished security [41]And he sat down opposite the treasury, and watched the multitude putting money into the treasury. Many rich people put in large sums. [42]And a poor widow came, and put in two copper coins, which make a penny. [43]And he called his disciples to him, and said to them, "Truly, I say to you, this poor widow has put in more than all those who are contributing to the treasury. [44]For they all contributed out of their abundance; but she out of her poverty has put in everything she had, her whole living."

11.27-33 and 12.13-44 *Ibid.*

Notes: These passages show Jesus playing Messiah, resorting to combative rhetoric in attempting to undermine the idea of religious office. The assumptions of his approach are valid: In the radical anarchism of the Rule of God, there are no hierarchs interposed between God and humans. For anyone in a spiritual fellowship to seek to dominate other members is the height of mental drunkenness. It usurps the rule of God and brings down God's wrath in the enmity and conflict such domination causes. Valid though his arguments may be, Jesus has again ignored the first step in recovery. Instead of inviting the authorities to acknowledge their illness and begin following the Twelve, he drunkenly attacks the wrongness of office. Rather than *metanoia*, his approach evokes defensiveness and hostility.

Sham authority: in countering their question about his own authority with a question about John's baptisms that they fear to answer, Jesus exposes the officials' authority for what it is, fear-based sham.

Temporality: by omitting reference to payments to the Temple treasury, Jesus seems to be saying that persons who render to religious authorities do so as if to Caesar, and their gifts, however charitable their use, are temporal not spiritual.

No privileged knowledge: Jesus explodes the idea that clergymen have knowledge about the afterlife that is unavailable to other people. For the idea of a general endtime resurrection he substitutes the view that each physical death is a simultaneous transition to heavenly life, citing God's assertion that he is God of the living not of the dead as proof that long-gone figures such as Abraham, Isaac, and Jacob are alive now, not lying dead somewhere awaiting a resurrection.

Unrenounced offices: to the scribe who reaffirms the Shema and the rule of neighborly love, Jesus says "You are not far from the Rule of God." What blocks the scribe's experience of *metanoia* is his failure to renounce the illusion of empowerment arising from his religious position. Jesus reinforces this attack on office by an exegesis of Ps 110.1 to the effect that, because he will be not Davidic but spiritual, the Messiah will have no need of official minions.

Veniality: pride and pomposity are faults, but the personal attack here is more an indicator of Jesus' drunken anger than of the spiritual shortcomings of the scribes.

Unrelinquished security: Christian Mark has Jesus speak this parable to the disciples, but in actuality it would have culminated his verbal assault on the priests and scribes. Its point is clear: the way to surrender self is to give up reliance on whatever one holds as one's dearest security. In the parable this was the widow's copper coins, which symbolize the authorities' privileged religious offices. In short, Jesus is challenging the priests and scribes to renounce their clerical status.

But Jesus' attack on the concept of hierarchical religion, drunken but no less rhetorically brilliant, does not change a single mind. By acting the part of a fanatical Galilean messiah, Jesus only increases the resolve of the frightened Jerusalem hierarchs to resist and retaliate.

PART V: SOBRIETY

The Markan narrative has reached its climax. Jesus has come to the definitive turning point of his recovery. He now realizes that his Jordan experience was provisional, that powerlessness over alcohol unaccompanied by the surrender of self leads only to mental drunkenness, harm to others, and a resumption of drinking. Addiction is that implacable. Yet the surest remedy for drinking is drink itself. Having drunk again and suffered further, Jesus is now ready to give himself unconditionally into the care of God—not just his drinking problem but his will and his life. The effects of this redemptive grace are manifest in Jesus' apocalypse (13.1-37), his message about wine at the Last Supper (14.22-25), his self-sacrifice in Gethsemane (14.32-42), and his reply to the high priest (14.60-62).

Chapter thirteen reports the revelation Jesus experienced as he sobered up in Jerusalem. Alcoholics know that the remorse following a bout of drunkenness after a time of sobriety often inspires a deeper awareness of the importance of recovery. One can picture Jesus on the morning after, aware of his troubles with the religious leaders but even more shaken by the realization of the gravity of his illness, saying to himself, "What have I done? I know I'm not God, yet I've been suicidally playing God. I know I'm not a messiah, yet I've succumbed to messianism. I know the only person I can change is myself, yet I've resorted to lunatic violence and verbal combat trying to reform religious drinkers and the leaders of my faith. I know that recovery must begin with a desire to stop drinking, yet I've ignored that truth completely in approaching others." In this painful self-inventory, Jesus commences to experience the humiliation heralding stage two of sobriety. Not surprisingly, it is also a time of apocalyptic insight.

Central to Jesus' revelation is a recognition that his problem is not Temple drinkers or the Jewish officials or even his own raging messianism; his problem is wine. For him as for any addict, wine wherever drunk, in religious ritual or otherwise, is the source of his troubles. It is, in the phrase he takes from the Book of Daniel, "the desolating abomination" (verse 14a from Dn 12.11). On seeing wine thus, persons should turn from drink to God (verse 14c). Drinkers will, like Jesus, suffer while awaiting insight (verses 5-13); they cannot know in advance the day or hour of its coming (verse 32), and must not expect that a messiah will solve their problem for them (verses 6 and 21-22). Yet Jesus does not label wine an objective evil. Rather, each individual must recognize its evil *for oneself*—"When *you* see the desolating abomination," Jesus says, whereupon the Markan narrator underscores the point, "Let the reader understand!" (verse 14b).

Chapter fourteen reports what Jesus says and does at the Last Supper and in Gethsemane, in consequence of these apocalyptic insights. Concluding that all religious drinkers are addicts unaware, he recognizes that the purpose of Passover wine (and projectively, Christian Eucharistic drinking) is to quicken in others the same awareness he has just experienced, to enable them to see wine as the source of their troubles, then to admit their powerlessness, quit drinking, and come into the Rule of God, all without having to suffer the pain and degradation experienced by advanced addicts. At the Supper, therefore, Jesus wordlessly offers the cup to others (verse 23) so that those who need to drink more can do so and those who have arrived at the turning point can experience their apocalypse. Next he identifies wine as the cause of his own troubles (verse 24a) yet also as the means of salvation (verse 24b), and as the drink he therefore pours out for the recovery of many (verse 24c). Finally he announces his own decision to drink no more (verse 25).

Thereafter it is Gethsemane, not Golgotha, that is the crux of Jesus' story; for there he sacrifices his agonistic self upon the ground before God, then arises a redeemed and truly human being. In so doing, Jesus both experiences and models the death of self that, after quitting drinking, is the source of sobriety. He asks for help in surrendering (verse 35) to the God of his understanding (verse 36a), admits his powerlessness over all things (verse 36b), and requests the removal of his cup addiction (verse 36c) not by his willpower but by God's (verse 36d). Later in Jerusalem, during his interrogation by the Jewish council, Jesus witnesses to the Messianic nature of Markôs recovery (verse 62). With this, Sobriety Mark comes to an end.

For instead of crucifixion, it is reasonable to believe, and to think of the Markans as believing, that Jesus had simply walked away from Jerusalem and returned to Galilee, where he lived out his life quietly and anonymously. Presumably the religious officials concluded that Jesus was neither a claimant to Messiahship nor a political insurrectionist but only a provincial drunkard, a man with particular religious beliefs and a certain following but otherwise not a danger. Of the Markôs fellowship they knew little or nothing. Presumably they told Jesus to return to Galilee and stay out of trouble, and presumably he did. Twice Mark recalls Jesus' expressed intention "to go before you to Galilee" (14.28 and 16.7).

Hangover Apocalypse (13.1-37)

13 . . . [3]And as Jesus sat on the Mount of Olives opposite the Temple, Peter and James and John and Andrew questioned him about his revelation, [4]"Tell us when *the turning point* will be. What will be the sign when all things *required for sobriety* are to be completed?" [5]And Jesus began to say to them, "Take heed that no one leads you astray. [6]Many will come in my name saying that I, *Jesus*, am Messiah, and they will lead many astray. [7]And when you hear of fighting and warfare, do not be disturbed, for that comes with *the addictive illness*, but the end is not yet. . . . [13]And you will be despised by all for being addicts just as I am despised. But whoever endures to the end will be saved.

[14]"Now, when you recognize the abomination that makes desolation as *the Passover cup* placed where it ought not to be [let the reader understand: *"the cup placed where it ought not to be" is the cup raised to be drunk*], then let all Jews flee *from wine* to the Rule of God. [15]Let him who is on the housetop not go down, nor enter his house to take anything away; [16]and let him who is in the field not turn back to take his mantle. . . .

[19]"In the days *before the turning point* there will be such horrible fighting as has not been from the beginning. . . . [20]And if the Lord had not shortened the days *to each one's*

changing of mind, no human being would be saved; but for the sake of the chosen ones, those whom he has chosen *for recovery*, he has shortened the days. [21]And if anyone says to you *of anyone at all, including me*, 'Look, here is the Messiah!' or 'Look, there he is!' do not believe it. [22]False Messiahs and false prophets will arise and show signs and wonders, to lead astray, if possible, the chosen ones. [23]But take heed; I have told you all things beforehand. [24]In those days, after the cataclysm *of hitting bottom*, it will seem as if the sun and moon have darkened, [25]the stars have fallen, and the powers in the heavens have been shaken.

[26]"Then everyone will see recovering people going about with a heavenly aura and empowered by the Higher Power. [27]And God will send out these messengers and gather *into the Markôs fellowship* those he has chosen from the four winds, from the ends of the earth to the ends of heaven. [28]From the fig tree learn its lesson: as soon as its branch becomes tender and puts forth its leaves, you know that summer is near. [29]So also, when you see these things taking place, you know that *recovery* is near, at the very gates. [30]Truly I say to you, your lives will not end without all *I have told you about sobriety* happening. . . . [32]But of the day and the hour no one knows, not the messengers, not I, but only the Father. [33]So take heed and watch *for your turning point*, for you do not know when the time will come. [34]It is like a man going on a journey, when he leaves home and . . . commands the doorkeeper to be on the watch. [35]Watch therefore—for you do not know when the master of the house will come, in the evening, or at midnight, or at cockcrow, or in the morning—[36]lest he come suddenly and find you asleep. [37]And what I say to you I say to all: Watch!"

---

[1]And as he came out of the Temple, one of his disciples said to him, "Look, Teacher, what wonderful stones and what wonderful buildings!" [2]And Jesus said to him, "Do you see these great buildings? There will not be left here one stone upon another, that will not be thrown down."

[3]And as he sat on the Mount of Olives opposite the Temple, Peter and James and John and Andrew asked him privately, [4]"Tell us, when will all this be, and what will be the sign when these things are all to be accomplished?" [5]And Jesus began to say to them, "Take heed that no one leads you astray. [6]Many will come in my name, saying, 'I am he!' and they will lead many astray. [7]And when you hear of wars and rumors of wars, do not be alarmed; this must take place, but the end is not yet. [8]For nation will rise against nation, and kingdom against kingdom; there will be earthquakes in various places, there will be famines; this is but the beginning of the sufferings. [9]But take heed to yourselves; for they will deliver you up to councils; and you will be beaten in synagogues; and you will stand before governors and kings for my sake, to bear testimony before them. [10]And the gospel must first be preached to all nations. [11]And when they bring you to trial and deliver you up, do not be anxious beforehand what you are to say; but say whatever is given you in that hour, for it is not you who speak, but the Holy Spirit. [12]And brother will deliver up brother to death, and the father his child, and children will rise against parents and have them put to death; [13]and you will be hated by all for my name's sake. But he who endures to the end will be saved.

[14]"But when you see the desolating sacrilege set up where it ought not to be [let the reader understand], then let those in Judea flee to the mountains. [15]Let him who is on the housetop not go down, nor enter his house, to take anything away; [16]and let him who is in the field not turn back to take his mantle. [17]And alas for those who are with child and for those who give suck in those days! [18]Pray that it may not happen in winter.

[19]"For in those days there will be such tribulation as has not been seen from the beginning of the creation which God created until now, and never will be. [20]And if the Lord had not shortened the days, no human being would be saved; but for the sake of the elect, whom he chose, he shortened the days. [21]And then if anyone says to you, 'Look, here is the Christ!' or 'Look, there he is!' do not believe it. [22]False Christs and false prophets will arise and show signs and wonders, to lead astray, if possible, the elect. [23]But take heed; I have told you all things beforehand. [24]But in those days, after the tribulation, the sun will be darkened, and the moon will not give its light, [25]and the stars will be falling from heaven, and the powers in the heavens will be shaken.

[26]"And then they will see the Son of man coming in clouds with great power and glory. 27-30 *Ibid.* [31]Heaven and earth will pass away, but my words will not pass away. 32-33 *Ibid.* [34]It is like a man going on a journey, when he leaves home and puts his servants in charge, each with

his work, and commands the doorkeeper to be on the watch." 35-37 *Ibid.*

Notes: Chapter thirteen presents Jesus' hangover revelation about the coming of sobriety. Camouflage of this topic was essential. Verses 1 and 2 in the canonical text are a contrivance prompting Christian readers to interpret the apocalypse as a prophecy of the fall of Jerusalem and destruction of the Temple, events that Mark knew would occur soon after he wrote. Viewed in this light, the key image in verse 14, the "desolating abomination," would seem to pertain, as in Daniel, to desecration of the Temple by foreign soldiery; and the admonition to flee would refer to escape from invaders, just as the imagery in verses 7-8 and 17-18 would refer to the ravages of war against the Romans. Verses 9-12 advising the faithful how to behave under persecution, as well as verse 31 and the "servant" clause in verse 34, appear to be the work not of Mark but of a Christian redactor. Behind the camouflage and redaction lies Jesus' vision of how the Messianic Markôs program, the Rule of God, comes to each addict and ultimately to the whole of addicted humanity.

The apocalypse has four parts. Part one, verses 3-8 and 13, introduces its topics: sign of the coming of sobriety; need to avoid messiahs; prospect of bitter fighting; certainty of being despised by presumed nonaddicts; and promise of final recovery. **About his revelation**: usually translated "privately," *kat idian* literally means "pertaining to his own." The phrase refers to the insights Jesus experienced while sobering up, which he has apparently mentioned earlier, in a general way, to his followers. **The turning point**: Mark's non-headed demonstrative *tauta*, "these (things)," is camouflage by lexical indefiniteness. **That I, Jesus, am Messiah**: "he" in verse 6 refers to Messiah. Christian versions fail to translate *hoti,* **that**, thus rendering "I am Messiah" a direct quotation wherein "I" refers to the speaker but not to Jesus. Translating *hoti* yields an indirect quotation, "that I am Messiah," an ambiguity in which "I" can refer either to the speaker or to Jesus. Knowing that "I" referred to Jesus, the Markans read the line, "many will come in my name calling me Messiah." Jesus foresees that persons soon to be called Christians will proclaim him Christ and thereby **lead many astray**, that is, away from the principles of recovery and into a cult of personality. His disavowal of Messiahship is repeated in verse 21, yet another ambiguity. **Comes with** translates *dei genesthai*, which means "happens as a necessary consequence." **Fighting and warfare**: what drinkers close to hitting bottom do is fight, everything and everyone. **Despised for being addicts**: here the despicable trait denoted by "the name of me" is

Jesus' addiction, hence that of the disciples.

Part two, verses 14-16 with replaced ellipses, identifies the sign of recovery as the realization that drink, epitomized by Passover wine, is the cause of one's troubles. Hence the ultimate joy of wine is not drinking it but deciding to leave it undrunk. This is the lesson the Markôs people drew from the undrunk Elijah cup at Passover—Elijah comes but drinks no wine. **When you recognize**: from *eidon*, to apprehend mentally, often in a new and unforeseen way. **Abomination**, *bdelugma*, connotes idolatry and generally refers to something esteemed by humans but hateful in the eyes of God. **That makes desolation**: the genitive *erēmōseōs* indicates that the abomination makes or leads to desolation. From the alcoholic perspective, a more incisive characterization of the ravages of wine is difficult to imagine. **Placed**: one of the senses of *histēmi*, usually translated standing or set up. The ambiguity of recognition in verse 14 turns on whether one sees a thing ordinarily thought to be an abomination in a place where it ought not be (the Christian reading, wherein the abomination is a pagan object intruded into the Temple confines) or whether one newly cognizes a thing in its ordinary place and ordinarily considered benign as an abomination (the sobriety reading, wherein the thing newly re-cognized is ritual wine). **Let the reader understand**: the narrator admonishes readers to interpret the sign for themselves. *Noeō*, translated "understand," refers to subjective knowledge known independently of perceptual or logical confirmation. The replaced ellipsis identifying **the Passover cup raised to be drunk** as **the abomination that makes desolation** reflects lore going back to Jesus and noetically (from *noeō*) accepted by Markôs people. Jesus had concluded that the sight of Passover wine about to be drunk, whether by oneself or fellow sederers, can trigger a changing of mind from drunken to sober thinking. This insight formed the basis of his theory of the purpose of ritual wine, a theory that he lays out in his discourse at the Last Supper. In 14.24a of the Supper narrative, Jesus enacts this recognition in his words over the wine, "this is my blood," which Markôs people understood to mean "this Passover wine is the cause of my bloodshed." The congruence of the sobriety readings of 13.14a and 14.24a supports the validity of each. **Flee from wine**: one's response to the revelation should be to turn at once from ritual drink to **the Rule of God**, represented by the "mountains" figure in the original Greek text. The admonitions to men **on the housetop** and **in the field** are parables underscoring the importance of immediate and decisive action upon recognizing the abomination of desolation.

Part three, verses 19-25, begins by mentioning the **fighting** that accompanies hitting bottom. Persons nearing the end of active addiction are at war, fighting drink, fighting others seeking to help, and fighting themselves. **Shortened the days** is Jesus' phrase for the grace of God given to those destined to recover before dying of their illness, whom Jesus calls **chosen ones**. It implies that seemingly nonaddicted religious drinkers as well as obvious addicts can expect an apocalypse before their affliction becomes terminal. As for **Messiah**, the replaced ellipsis **anyone at all including me** should be understood in contrast to the Christian version, "anyone other than me." Just as Jesus knew that he was not the Messiah, he also knew that messiahs in general, people who tell you what you should do or what they will do for you, cannot help addicts and cannot avoid **leading the chosen ones astray**. **After the cataclysm of hitting bottom** refers in stock apocalyptic imagery (**sun, moon, stars, powers**) to a time when persons look back after bottoming out and contemplate the surprising metanoia, the radical upheaval and reorganization, that has occurred in their thinking.

Part four, verses 26-37, first shows recovering sons of men twelfth-stepping newcomers into the Markôs program. It goes on to counsel awareness of the signs that recovery is near, to state that only God knows the exact time, and to stress the need for watchful waiting. In verse 26, traditionally understood to depict Christ descending from heaven on clouds, *ton huion tou anthrōpon*, literally "son of man," is once again read as the collective noun **recovering people**. **Going about** is one of the many meanings of *erchomai*, ordinarily translated "coming." Imputed realistically to persons, *nephelais*, clouds, coupled with *doxēs*, glory, would indicate **a heavenly aura**. To the Markans *meta dunameōs pollēs* would have denoted the power of God, hence the reading **empowered by the Higher Power**. Jesus is not talking about the descent from heaven of a solitary Messiah figure but the ubiquity of recovering people carrying the message here on earth. Exactly the same lexical considerations govern the translation of Jesus' reply to the high priest in 14.62, which is essentially identical to 13.26. **These messengers**, *tous angelous*, are recovering people sent by **God** to bring **the chosen** to wellness. The **lesson of the leafing fig tree** is to believe that one's turning point is near, that Jesus' words about sobriety will come to pass within each person's lifetime, although **no one but the Father** knows the exact day or hour. What each addict, what all addicted humanity, should do is **watch**—and continue to drink religiously until the time.

Wanted For Arrest (14.1-2)

14 [1]It was now two days before the Passover and the feast of Unleavened Bread. And the chief priests and the scribes were seeking how to arrest him by stealth, and kill him; [2]for they said, "Not during the feast, lest there be a tumult of the people."

1-2 *Ibid.*

Notes: Although sober, Jesus, like all recovering alcoholics, must face the consequences of his drunken actions.

Anointing in Sobriety (14.3-9)

[3]And while he was at Bethany in the house of Simon the leper, as he sat at table, a woman came with an alabaster jar of ointment of pure nard, very costly, and she broke the jar and poured it over his head. [4]But there were some who said to themselves indignantly, "Why was the ointment thus wasted? [5]For this ointment might have been sold for more than three hundred denarii, and given to the poor." And they reproached her. [6]But Jesus said, "Let her alone; why do you trouble her? She has done a beautiful thing . . . . [9]Truly, I say to you, wherever the wellness message is proclaimed in the whole world, what she has done will be told in memory of her."

3-6 *Ibid.* [7]"For you always have the poor with you, and whenever you will, you can do good to them; but you will not always have me. [8]She has done what she could; she has anointed my body beforehand for burying." 9 *Ibid.*

Notes: This allegorical scene depicts Mark's first use of woman/women to symbolize powerless recovering people. Later occasions are the upper (women's) room (14.15), the serving girl (14.66-69), and the women at the cross (15.40-41) and empty tomb (16.1-8). Here the woman expends not just part but all her costly ointment and does not just pour from but breaks her valuable jar. These actions symbolize repudiation of self, a sacrifice that leads to anointing in sobriety, and foreshadow Jesus' self-sacrifice in Gethsemane. Verses 7-8 are camouflage that shift the story's focus to anointing for burial.

Poured it over his head: *katacheō*, to pour down upon, contains the root *cheō*, to pour, which is lexically related to *chriō*, to anoint sacramentally. The latter is the Greek verb from which the English "Christ" derives and which translates the Hebrew verb for anointing from which the English "Messiah" derives. The Cupmasters would have interpreted the woman's anointing of the now sober Jesus essentially as a sacrament celebrating his sobriety, the **beautiful thing** which recovering people do in ratifying the wellness of another.

A Markôs Passover (14.12-17)

[12]And on the first day of Unleavened Bread, when they sacrificed the Passover lamb, his disciples said to him, "Where will you have us go and prepare for you to eat the Passover?" [13]And he sent two of his disciples, and said to them, "Go into the city, and a man carrying a jar of water will meet you; follow him, [14]and wherever he enters, say to the householder, 'The Teacher says, Where is my guest room, where I am to eat the Passover with my disciples?' [15]And he will show you a large upper room, *the room for women*, furnished and ready; there prepare for us." [16]And the disciples set out and went to the city, and found it as he had told them; and they prepared the Passover. [17]And when it was evening, Jesus came with the twelve *sobriety precepts*.

12-17 *Ibid*.

Notes: Beneath a guise of clandestine prearrangement similar to that surrounding the procurement of the donkey (11.1-7), Mark indicates that the Jerusalem seder, the Last Supper, was a Passover meeting of the Markôs fellowship. **A man carrying a jar of water** is the tipoff. The twin anomalies of a man doing what women do, carrying a jar or pitcher, and the contents of the jar being water not wine, signify the camouflaged intention. After the Jordan water drunk by Jesus (1.9-10) and the cup of water given Markôs newcomers (9.41), Passover water is the third of three water-not-wine emblems in Mark. The water carrier pointedly contrasts to the man carrying a skin of wine in I Samuel 10.3. **Guest room**, *kataluma*, literally a loosening place, a room where travelers loose their burdens and undo their clothing and sandals, is a wonderful term for a Twelve Step meeting room, where persons unburden themselves verbally.

An upper room, *anagaion*, literally a room above the ground and in Hellenic culture the room where women resided. **The room for women**: this filled ellipsis is another pointer to the identity of the Jerusalem supper as a Cupmaster meeting, since as just pointed out, women in the final chapters of Sobriety Mark symbolize recovering persons. **Came with the twelve sobriety precepts**: Unless one believes that the two disciples returned to Bethany only to double back to Jerusalem with Jesus and the other ten, **the twelve** unambiguously refers not to persons but to the Markans' twelve sobriety precepts, further evidence that the supper was a Markôs meeting.

The Message Embodied (14.22)

[22]And as they were eating, Jesus took bread, and blessed and broke it, and gave it to them. Then he said, "Pay attention, this is *the message* I embody."

---

[22]And as they were eating, he took bread, and blessed, and broke it, and gave it to them, and said, "Take; this is my body."

Notes: In verse 22, Jesus prefaces his discourse on wine by directing his hearers to pay attention to what he is about to say. This reading of the verse differs radically from the traditional version of Jesus' statement, which assumes that he is equating bread to his body. **This**, *touto*, is referentially ambiguous. A nonheaded demonstrative, it is ordinarily thought to refer to the matzo bread the speaker is distributing, but it can also refer to the speaker's upcoming utterance, to what he is about to say. The difference is that, for example, between someone holding a garment who says "this is my coat" and someone responding to a proposal who says "this is my answer." Recall that, for the Markans, **bread**, *artos,* symbolized Word of God. When said of bread construed symbolically, *sōma mou*, literally "my body," would mean **the message I embody**. Although absent from the New Testament, *ensōmatōsis*, "embodiment," occurs in both classical and patristic Greek and would have been available as a lexical concept to Mark and his Greek-speaking readers. **Pay attention** translates *labete*, which when said of a concrete object means "take" in the sense of grasp manually, but when said of an action or an utterance means "receive mentally" in the sense of attend, look, and/or listen. A gloss of verse 22 would read:

> Receive it in your mind, this that I am about to do and say, which the matzo morsel I am giving you symbolizes, is my embodiment, the message my words and actions embody.

So read, the verse creates an alternative context for interpreting the Supper narrative. In Christian Mark, the verse initiates Jesus' discourse on two substances of equal thematic import, bread and wine. In Sobriety Mark, however, Jesus calls attention to (verse 22), then delivers (verses 23-25), a discourse on wine alone. In the Christian version it is the sacrificial and commensal aspects of wine and bread that are significant. In the Sobriety gospel the focus is wine in all its aspects, from ritual drinking, to ruinous addictive drinking, to salvific drinking.

Discourse on Wine (14.23-26a)

[23]And he took a cup, and when he had given thanks he gave it to them *to drink or not drink as they chose.* And they all drank of it. [24]And he said to them, "This *wine* is *the cause of* my blood*shed yet also* covenant blood which I pour out for *the recovery of* many. [25]Truly, I say to you, I will drink no more of the fruit of the vine, not ritually and not otherwise, until the day I drink the new wine of the Rule of God." [26a]And then they sang Hallel.

---

[23]And he took a cup, and when he had given thanks he gave it to them, and they all drank of it. [24]And he said to them, "This is my blood of the covenant, which is poured out for many. [25]Truly, I say to you, I shall not drink again of the fruit of the vine until that day when I drink it new in the kingdom of God." [26a]And when they had sung a hymn. . .

Notes: Before witnessing his definitive renunciation of drink in his discourse on wine, Jesus wordlessly passes the cup to all present, thereby offering each person the choice of drinking or not drinking. He then voices his recognition of wine as the cause of his bloodshed, and announces his intention to quit drinking for good and to embrace instead the Rule of God. Between these utterances Jesus explains his understanding of the purpose of Passover wine. He describes wine not just as the cause of bloodshed but also, ironically, as the means to humanity's promised salvation, hence the drink prescribed by God for the many.

Verse 23: In terms of semantic function, **he gave it to them**, *edōken autois*, is either a command or an offer. Christians interpret the clause as a command to drink. The Markans, by contrast, understood Jesus to have believed that ritual drinking must be presented as a free choice, an offer with no implication of command, so that people at the powerless point might decline to drink, while those still awaiting their apocalypse might be free to partake and so come nearer to their own crisis time. Hence the restored ellipsis: **to drink or not drink as they chose**. The disciples' response to the offer, **and they all drank of it**, reflects Mark's view of these men as active addicts destined to drink still more.

Verse 24 is based upon three implied clauses: this wine is my blood, this wine is covenant blood, and I pour out this wine for many. **My bloodshed**: The first clause has either a performative or an epiphanal function. Christians construe it as the former, understanding the words to change the wine in the cup into blood from Jesus' veins. The Markans, however, construed them as conveying an epiphany, as depicting the moment a drinker, here Jesus, recognizes wine as the *cause* of his bloodshed, the *source* of his troubles. In that sense the statement is a metaphor, technically a metonymy, that equates wine and blood in a causal relationship signfying the carnage associated with drink. It is the shock of this recognition, a recognition known to former alcohol addicts in every age, that stamps the utterance as epiphanal. The clause is also thematically ambiguous. Christians understand Jesus to be speaking about his sacrificed blood, which persons can share in an unbloody way by drinking liturgical wine, whereas the Markans understood Jesus to be speaking about wine, all wine, liturgical and otherwise, as both the cause of and a figure for real bloodshed. Accordingly, both **blood**, *haima*, and **is**, *estin*, are lexically ambiguous. The Christian sense of "is" is transubstantiational; its Sobriety sense is causal. The Christian sense of "blood" is veinous blood given by Jesus in the form of wine; its Sobriety sense is shed blood, blood Jesus has previously and/or may again spill as a consequence of drink.

Covenant: the second clause, "this wine is covenant blood," juxtaposes divinely promised sobriety and the alcoholic perdition depicted in the first clause. The ambiguity is in the conjunctive relationship implicit between the two clauses. Christians understood the connection as a simple additive relationship, "my blood *and* covenant blood," whereas the Markans discerned a contrastive as well as an additive relationship, "my blood *yet also* covenant blood." **Yet also** reflects the irony of sobriety following addiction, namely, that the wine that casts drinkers down to the depths of dissolution (*haima mou* in the Greek) is the same wine that ultimately lifts them up to the heights of covenanted sobriety (*haima diathēkēs*).

Poured out: the third clause, "I pour out this wine for many," contains an ambiguity of figure in the passive *ekchunnomenon*, "is poured out." The Christian reading construes pouring as a metaphor foreshadowing Jesus' blood shed in crucifixion, which the many are to drink as a way of sharing vicariously in his death. The Sobriety reading understands pouring literally, as wine poured for ritual drinkers to drink and so hit bottom en route to sobriety, and also symbolically, as message poured forth from the speaker revealing the ironic connection between drinking and recovery. **For many**, *huper pollōn*, extends the offer of sobriety from the few who are obviously addicted to all other ritual drinkers. Jesus took this phrase from Second Isaiah's Suffering Servant poem (Is 52.13-53.12). As discussed in connection with 10.40-45, the Markôs people believed the Servant a derelict drunkard who suffers as vicarious addiction bearer for the many, the so-called normal drinkers in any society, then "gives himself as a guilt offering" (Is 53.10) thereby showing the multitudes the path to atonement short of the extremes he and other public drunkards endure. A gloss of verse 24 would read:

> I now recognize wine, ritual and otherwise, as the cause of my bloodshed yet also, metaphorically, as the blood of our sobriety covenant, whose irony I now reveal and which I have poured out as drink leading to the recovery of all who partake.

A similar understanding of wine as ironically salvific can be heard in the pithy wisdom of alcoholics, "If I'd never started to drink, I'd never have gotten sober." Persons who think a sip of Communion wine insufficient to bring drinkers to the turning point should bear in mind that hitting bottom is an act of God and not a function of quantity drunk.

Verse 25, invariably omitted from Christian Eucharistic formulas, conveys the final element of Jesus' message about wine. It articulates the most important words a powerless alcoholic can speak: **I will drink no more**. **New wine**: the grammatical ambiguity in *heōs . . . auto pinō kainon* permits translation of the adjective *kainon*, "new," not only as a complement or an adverbial (until I drink it new/anew) but also as a prenominal adjective. Literally this would be "until . . . I drink new it;" but because English does not permit adjectives to modify pronouns, the noun wine must be substituted for the pronoun, yielding "until . . . I drink new wine." The "new wine" version, in turn, contains an ambiguity of reference. The question is, is "it" or "wine," whichever is chosen, coreferential with **fruit of the vine**, or disjunct? That is, is the speaker referring to the same wine named twice or to two different wines? The answer depends on which version of the grammatical ambiguity is selected. In "I will drink no more of the fruit of the vine until I drink it new/anew in the Rule of God," fruit of the vine and it refer to the same wine named twice, real wine drunk in ritual and then in the Rule of God. In "I will drink no more of the fruit of the vine until I drink the new wine of the Rule of God," however, the reference is not to one wine named then rementioned by a pronoun but rather to two different wines, real Passover wine then something different, wine of a special character peculiar to the Rule of God. Hence the question: does *oinos . . . kainon* refer literally to wine of a certain kind (*oinos neos*, for example, would mean wine recently produced), or is it a metaphor referring to something quite different, sobriety described oxymoronically in terms of actual wine drinking? Cupmasters interpreted the phrase in the latter way, as a metaphor for recovery. **Rule of God**, of course, is the Markôs program. **No more . . . not ritually . . . not otherwise** aims to capture the emphatic triple negative of the Greek. The gloss of verse 25 would read:

> Truly I say to you, henceforth I will drink no more of the fruit of the vine—not wine drunk ritually nor wine on any other occasion —until that day when I drink the new wine of the Rule of God, my figure for sobriety in the Cupmaster fellowship.

Jesus may have based his disavowal on Psalm 16.4b-5, wherein an ancient Canaanite convert to Yahwism renounces his pagan wine liturgy in order to drink the metaphorical "smooth wine" of Yahweh:[10]

> (Ps 16.4b) Surely I will no longer pour libations to them [the false wine gods] from my hands, nor will I again raise their names to my lips [drink wine in their service].
>
> (5) O Yahweh, you have portioned out my cup of smooth wine, you yourself have made falling low [hitting bottom] my lot.

Verse 26a: The Passover supper concluded with the entire company **singing Hallel**, Psalms 115-118. Psalm 116 would have had special meaning for Jesus and his followers. *Mark As Recovery Story* interprets this psalm, generally considered the gratitude song of a person whom Yahweh has cured of sickness, as bearing the earmarks of an alcoholic's recovery story: the psalmist suffers a degrading illness, hits his low point, admits defeat, calls out for help, recognizes that only a power greater than man's can save him, drinks "the cup of God's salvation" instead of wine, and witnesses to his recovery in the court of Yahweh's house.[11] Verses 10 and 16 of the psalm would seem to explain Jesus' experience of a sense of sonship at the Jordan (Mk 1.11):

> (Ps 116.16) O Yahweh, truly I am your servant. I am your

servant, your faithful son; you have loosed my fetters!

The phrase "your faithful son" echoes verse 10 of the psalm, "In faith I acted, even though it was to admit 'I am powerless . . . .'"[12] This suggests that the admission of powerlessness as a faith action is the criterion of sonship.

In summary, what transpires at the Last Supper is humanity's turn from mortal illness to a program of wellness and life. At the seder, Jesus as quintessential recovering addict identifies alcohol as both actual and symbolic cause of his troubles, then announces his intention to stop drinking and give himself to the Rule of God. He also voices his understanding of liturgical drink, namely, that alcohol is not just foe but also friend, the agent not just of perdition but of salvation, and is therefore to be drunk religiously until the time when it is no longer to be drunk at all, for it will have brought the drinker to his or her turning point. Finally, the co-addicted disciples assume their role as prototypical ministers ordained to model liturgical drinking. They dutifully drink the proffered wine and await their turn to offer the cup to the many.

Gethsemane Surrender (14.32-42a)

[32]And they went to a place which was called Gethsemane; and he said to his disciples, "Sit here while I pray." [33]And he took with him Peter and James and John, and he began to be amazed and strangely awestruck. [34]And he said to them, "My self is sorrowful as it approaches death. Remain here and watch *me*." [35]And going a little farther, he fell on the ground and prayed for the strength to get through the moment at hand. [36]Then he said, "Abba (Father), as you have all powers, *so I am powerless*; take away my cup *addiction*, but not through my willing it but by your willing it." [37]Next he came and found them sleeping. And he said to Peter, "Simon, are you asleep? Could you not watch *me* one hour? [38]Watch *my actions*, and pray that you may be spared having to learn the hard way what happens when your spirit is willing but your body remains inert." [39]So again he went away and prayed, saying the same words. [40]And again he came and found them sleeping, for their eyes were burdened down and they did not know how they should

respond to his actions. [41]And he came the third time, and said to them, "Are you still sleeping and avoiding action? Such is enough to have brought to pass the hour of my betrayal into the hands of those who err. [42a]*But still I say, arise!*"

---

[32]And they went to a place which was called Gethsemane; and he said to his disciples, "Sit here while I pray." [33]And he took with him Peter and James and John, and he began to be greatly distressed and troubled. [34]And he said to them, "My soul is very sorrowful, even to death; remain here, and watch." [35]And going a little farther, he fell on the ground and prayed that, if it were possible, the hour might pass from him. [36]And he said, "Abba, Father, all things are possible to thee; remove this cup from me; yet not what I will, but what thou wilt." [37]And he came and found them sleeping, and he said to Peter, "Simon, are you asleep? Could you not watch one hour? [38]Watch and pray that you may not enter into temptation; the spirit indeed is willing, but the flesh is weak." [39]And again he went away and prayed, saying the same words. [40]And again he came and found them sleeping, for their eyes were very heavy; and they did not know what to answer him. [41]And he came the third time, and said to them, "Are you still sleeping and taking your rest? It is enough; the hour has come; the Son of man is betrayed into the hands of sinners. [42a]Rise, let us be going."

Notes: In Gethsemane Jesus undergoes the sacrifice of self required for lasting sobriety. Christians have always understood the Gethsemane narrative to mean that Jesus wavered in his resolve and prayed that he might be spared his destined ordeal. Markans, on the other hand, fully aware of the text's ambiguities, knew that Jesus, although momentarily sad at the imminence of self death, had not lost his nerve but had prayed for help in making his surrender, then had admitted his powerlessness and asked for removal of his addiction to the cup, by God's will not his. Jesus hoped that the disciples would watch his surrender and follow suit; but as drinkers still unready to stop drinking, they cannot comprehend his actions. Thus they betray Jesus' self sacrifice and set the stage for the development of a religion based on self will and the idea of a substitutionary rather than a wayshowing atonement.

The name **Gethsemane** is believed by some scholars to be formed of the Greek *sēmeion*, meaning sign, and the Hebrew/Aramaic *gat*, meaning press. It has been said that the press at this location may have been a wine press. If so, how fitting that Jesus' self-sacrifice should have occurred at a place called the Sign of the Winepress.[13]

Verses 32-34: **Amazed and awestruck** convey Mark's descriptions of the emotions he believed Jesus experienced on the threshold of his encounter with God. RSV's "distressed and troubled" reflect the Christian idea that Jesus had panicked and wavered in purpose. *Psuchē*, a term first-century readers would have understood as soul or inner being, names what the modern world calls **self**, in Jesus' case the overly individuated, auto-empowered self that has animated his drunken career from Caesarea Philippi to Jerusalem. The **sorrow** Jesus acknowledges is the sadness many feel at the turning point, the **death** of one's old addictive self. **Watch**, traditionally interpreted "be on lookout for my captors," means "watch me, look at my surrender." **The ground** to which Jesus falls is the same ground from which Adam and Eve first rose up in their Edenic rebellion against God, thus the place appointed for human atonement. There Jesus, who has stopped playing God and renounced his messianic hubris, asks for help in making his oblation.

Verse 35: Perhaps more than any other in the gospel, this verse is key to a Markan understanding of Jesus' spirituality. Any translation of the verse must consider the referents of "hour," the status of *dunaton* as a weakened or a fully lexicalized predicate, and the dual meanings of *parerchomai*. Although ordinarily assumed to refer to the time of Jesus' upcoming trial and execution, "hour" can just as readily refer to **the moment at hand**, to the present time in Gethsemane. Readers have always believed that Jesus was distraught at the approach of death, and that the death he had in mind was crucifixion. Not necessarily. It can also be the **death of self**, *hē psuchē mou heōs thanatou* of verse 34, a death about to occur even as he speaks. The ambiguities in *dunatos* and *parerchomai* are crucial. *Ei dunaton estin* is a present tense indicative understood as a prayer requesting a desired outcome, "if (*ei*) possible (*dunaton*) it is (*estin*)." But translating the adjective *dunaton* as "possible" weakens the request for power so important at this juncture. In discussing Mark's uses of *dunamai* and *thelō* in weakened senses as the auxiliaries could and would, scholars point out that translators must decide from context when these words carry their full lexical meanings and when they are weakened.[14] For Mark, a central issue in the gospel is power and who has it, man or God. The idea that Jesus in verse 35 might be acknowledging lack of power by asking for help is obscured when *dunaton* is weakened to "possible." The phrase can just as correctly be understood as a prayer to be empowered, to receive *dunamis*. Hence an alternate reading, with *ei* rendered "might," *dunaton* given its full lexical value, and the implied dative "to him" supplied, would be: "prayed that it might be powerfulled [to him]." The awkward English can be smoothed by substituting the phrase "to be empowered" or its idiomatic equivalent, **for the strength. To get through**: *parerchomai*, a verb with many senses, has the meaning "to pass by in time" or "elapse." Hence, in addition to the familiar readings, pass him by or pass from him, that is, not happen to him, idiomatically, that he not have to go through it, *hina . . . parelthe ap autou he hōra* can also read, that . . . the hour elapse from him. English idioms for this meaning would be to get through a situation, to get it behind one or get it over with. Combining these alternative understandings produces the literal reading, "prayed that it might be powerfulled to him that the present moment elapse from him," which may be idiomatically rendered, **prayed for the strength to get through the moment at hand**. Obviously, verse 35 so read is *not* requesting a change of destiny. Jesus' purpose in Gethsemane is *not* wavering. He is *not* asking to be spared the ordeal of an ominous hour. Rather, he is asking God's help to make the surrender he will enact in verse 36.

Verse 36, in turn, liberated from the context set by verse 35 as ordinarily translated, now reveals its identity as a self-repudiating surrender. For spiritual surrender and not a wish to avoid suffering is what the remainder of the recontextualized prayer recounts. First is an alternative understanding of the referent of "cup." Here Mark exploits an ambiguity not of lexical sense but of figure. The traditional view treats "cup" as a fixed expression referring to one's destiny, and considers "remove this cup from me" a repetition of Jesus' request for a change of fortune. But to Markôs people, who had known a removal of the cup from their own lives, "cup" functioned as an active metaphor figuring the addictive illness that has brought Jesus to this moment. It is the cup of his question to the disciples (10.38), "Can you drink the cup I am drinking?" And it is the twofold cup described by Second Isaiah (see page xii above) and indicative of both mental and physical drunkenness, "the cup of anger and the chalice of drunkenness," a cup given by God (Is 51.17-21), removed by God (Is 51.22), then handed to others who practice domination (Is 51.23). In short, it is a cup that Jesus, like all addicts with a desire for sobriety, most earnestly wishes to have removed. Hence the translation, **take away my cup addiction**.

Second, the statement *panta dunata soi*, **you have all powers**, represents Jesus' rejection of the illusion of self-empowerment. The root *dunamis* refers to spiritual power emanating from God without which humans remain hostage to their angst. *Dunamis* allays fear, quiets anger, heals illness, dispels addiction, and lifts the compulsion to judge, fight, and control. To persons who have known spiritual surrender, Jesus' prayer highlights the central truth of Gethsemane: *dunamis* flows from God when humans admit they lack it utterly. Until then, we refuse to acknowledge our powerlessness. The familiar translation of *panta dunata soi*, "all things are possible to thee," though grammatical, fails to capture the sense of Jesus' words as a recognition of his own lack of power. To persons who exalt Jesus as an idealized figure on whom to project an unrecognized belief in their own self-empowerment, this understanding may seem threatening. But to those who have known the conviction of powerlessness and see in Jesus' prayer a type of their own experience, **as you have all powers so I am powerless** is the masterstroke of Jesus' entire career.

Third is the petition ordinarily rendered, "yet not what I will, but what thou wilt." Generally said to indicate Jesus' repudiation of a desire ("what I wish") or resignation to an outcome, it can just as readily express his renunciation of self-will as a power source. From the outset, Jesus has resorted to ever increasing willfulness in attempting to realize his vision for the world, the Rule of God. In Gethsemane, he admits defeat in his battle of wills with God, acknowledging that the "cup" of self can be removed only by an other, only by God's dunamis and not his own. Thus the final petition reads, **but not through my willing it but your willing it**. Taken together, Jesus' three prayer petitions—admission of powerlessness, request for removal of his cup addiction, and renunciation of self-will—signal the beginning of the end of humanity's primordial rebellion against God and of the addictive illness that issues from it.

Verses 37-42a: The disciples' **sleeping** is both a symbol of their spiritually unawake condition and the real consequence of Passover wine. The idiomatic **having to learn the hard way** translates *peirasmos*, an ordeal by suffering. It refers to the pain experienced by addicts who say they wish to recover but refuse to act, who say they need help but will not ask for it, will not take the action necessary to receive it. It is characteristic alcoholic behavior, observable in the disciples' asthenia. **Again he prayed, saying the same words**: in praying twice, Jesus may have asked first for release from physical drunkenness and then for freedom from mental drunkenness. The two requests would have led to stages one and two of sobriety. **Avoiding action** comes from *anapauō*, inactivity or inaction. **Such is enough** translates *apechō*, a formulaic verb used to signify receipt of full payment, in modern parlance, "received in full." **My betrayal**: here "son of man" refers to Jesus and the principles of recovery he embodies. **Those who err** is the root meaning of *hamartōlōn*, ordinarily rendered "sinners." **Arise**: Jesus makes a last attempt to rouse the narcotized disciples, to no avail. The idea is that the disciples' unresponsiveness to Jesus' self-sacrifice betrays his witness. Mark is not speaking so much about Peter and James and John as about the rising Christian clergy forty years later, who, he believes, are promoting a spirituality inimical to that of the Markôs movement.

As portrayed in Sobriety Mark, Gethsemane is the real locus of the atonement miracle Christians celebrate at Easter. There Jesus, released from the twin bondage of alcohol and self, arises from the ground a humbled man in a redeemed Eden, no longer a pretender to Godlike autonomy but a true child of God and son of man. In shaping the Gethsemane narrative, Mark knew that his Judean Christian audience would project into their reading an auto-empowered Jesus Messiah, a paragon who briefly falters but then heroically accepts crucifixion. But he also knew that members of the Markôs fellowship, recognizing the ambiguities and believing that it was Gethsemane and not a Roman cross that had concluded their founder's career, would see in his text the surrendered Jesus whom they memorialized as wayshowing archetype of the redemptive humility they sought in recovery.

Messianic Profession (14.46-50, 53-62)

46Then they laid hands on him and seized him. 47But one of those who stood by drew his sword, and struck the slave of the high priest and cut off his ear. 48And Jesus said to them, "Have you come out as against a robber, with swords and clubs to capture me? 49Day after day I was with you in the Temple teaching, and you did not seize me. . . ." 50And *his disciples* all forsook him, and fled. 53And they led Jesus to the high priest; and all the chief priests and the elders and the scribes were assembled. . . . 55Now the chief priests and the whole council sought testimony against Jesus to put him to death; but they found none. 56For many bore false witness against him, and their witness did not agree. 57And some stood up and bore false witness against him, saying, 58"We heard him say, 'I will destroy this temple that is made with hands, and shortly thereafter build another not made with hands.'" 59Yet not even so did their testimony agree. 60And the high priest stood up in the midst, and asked Jesus, "Have you no answer to make? What is it that these men testify against you?" [61]But he was silent and made no answer. Again the high priest asked him, "Are you the Messiah, the son of the Blessed?" [62]And Jesus said, "*Only in the sense that* you will see other sober people besides me empowered by God and going about with a heavenly aura."

46-53 *Ibid.* [49]". . . But let the scriptures be fulfilled." [54]And Peter had followed him at a distance, right into the courtyard of the high priest; and he was sitting with the guards, and warming himself at the fire. 55-61 *Ibid.* [62]And Jesus said, "I am; and you will see the Son of man sitting at the right hand of Power, and coming with the clouds of heaven."

Notes: The Markans remembered that Jesus had been apprehended and interrogated by the Jerusalem leaders before being sent home to Galilee. His serene demeanor here contrasts with the drunken anger and contentiousness of his assault on Temple drinkers and the religious authorities. **I was with you in the Temple teaching**: this surprising utterance, inconsistent with his actual behavior in the Temple, suggests that Jesus may have acted in a blackout of which he had no memory. **And his disciples . . . fled**: knowing that Jesus would be found an inebriate, the disciples, portrayed by Mark as prototypes of a Christian clergy scandalized by the idea of a drunkard Messiah, abandon him completely. Verse 54, incompatible with verse 50, is a device in Christian Mark ascribing Petrine attestation to Jesus' Messianic profession. **I will destroy this temple** is a saying by Jesus contrasting his old self-willed life **made with hands** to his new life after spiritual awakening; **not made with hands** means made by the Spirit.

Are you the Messiah: Mark writes "Christ," but the high priest would have used the Hebrew term. As for Jesus' answer, manuscripts of Mark vary between the absolute "I am" and "you say that I am." The latter accords with the noncommittal versions in Matthew ("You have said so") and Luke ("You say that I am"). **Only in the sense that**: the restored ellipsis is a reminder that the sober Jesus believed Messiah to be not a person but the principles of spiritual living embodied in the Twelve and other aspects of the Markôs program. Jesus had discerned these principles in Psalms 16 and 116, in Elijah's waterdrinking, in the witness of Second Isaiah's Suffering Servant, and in the four cups of wine drunk entire in the post-exilic Passover rite. He had seen them in the power of the Rule of God manifest throughout his Galilean career and on this very night, at the Supper and Gethsemane. The most he could claim was to have been chosen as founder and exemplar of the

Cupmaster movement.

The remainder of Jesus' response (verse 62) is an almost verbatim reprise of 13.26. "Son of Man" is rendered by the collective phrase **other sober people besides me**, people recovering in the Markôs fellowship. **Going about**, coming and going carrying the message, translates *erchomai*. **Heavenly aura**: *nephelōn tou ouranon*, "clouds of heaven," refers to the aura which newcomers to sobriety often say they observe surrounding twelfth-steppers. For the final time in the gospel, Jesus proclaims the Messianic status not of himself alone but of the Cupmaster program and all who carry its message to other addicts.

Return to Galilee (14.28; 16.7)

14.28*Jesus said*, "But after I am raised up, I will go before you to Galilee."

16.7*And the young man in the tomb said to the women*, "But go, tell his disciples and Peter that he is going before you in Galilee; there you will see him, as he told you."

14.28 and 16.7 *Ibid.*

Notes: Once again, the position here is that the Markans believed that Jesus was not crucified but had been released as a harmless drunkard, unaccountably sober on Passover night, and had quietly returned to Galilee. This is not to say that there was no crucifixion in Jerusalem at Passover of 30 A.D., only that the identity of the victim is disputable. This topic is examined further in the Afterword (p. 115).

In 14.28, **raised up** comes from *egeirō*, to awaken, arise, be resurrected. Christians read this statement as a reference to Jesus' resurrection after crucifixion and physical death, whereas the Markans applied it to his resurrection from the ground of Gethsemane, after *psuchē* death and spiritual rebirth, where Jesus uses *egeirō* (14.42) in admonishing the sleeping disciples to undergo the same dying and rising he has just experienced. Apparently Markôs people saw no need for the crucifixion of anyone, rather for spiritual surrender and rebirth by everyone. In 16.7, **Galilee** contrasts with Jerusalem, the latter symbolizing the willful and often angry strife typical of religion, the former the serenity characteristic of sobriety.

PART VI: PROPHETIC ALLEGORIES

Markôs people knew that many of Jesus' original followers, after his disappearance, had betrayed the principles of their sobriety program by drinking again and denying Jesus' identity as a wine addict. They came to believe that it was Jesus rather than an unknown insurrectionist who was crucified, and together with nonaddicts began to speak of him as a resurrected Messiah and founder of the Christian movement. Soon the infant churches had succeeded in encrypting the real Jesus story within a counter-Markan spirituality which Markôs people, in their frankly sardonic version of the *petras*/Peter pun, figuratively labeled a rock tomb. Mark, however, believed that a time would come when, allegorically speaking, Jesus would escape the tomb and return to Galilee, symbolic locus of a revived Cupmaster fellowship. Thus he ended his gospel with narratives which provided Christians with the detailed passion story they expected, and at the same time informed Markôs people, allegorically, of the betrayal and prophetic future of their movement. Part VI, essentially an appendix to Sobriety Mark, consists of nine prophetic allegories, as translated in RSV: Betrayal, Stricken Shepherd, Denial, Barabbas or Barnasha, Crucifixion, Rock Tomb, Women, Young Man in White, and Very Early on the Third Day.

Betrayal (14.10-11, 18-21, 42b-45)

[10]Then Judas Iscariot, who was one of the Twelve, went to the chief priests in order to betray him to them. [11]And when they heard it they were glad, and promised to give him money. And he sought an opportunity to betray him. . . . [18]And as they were at table eating, Jesus said, "Truly, I say to you, one of you will betray me, one who is eating with me." [19]They began to be sorrowful, and to say to him one after another, "Is it I?" [20]He said to them, "It is one of the twelve, one who is dipping bread in the same dish with me. [21]For the Son of man goes as it is written of him, but woe to that man by whom the Son of man is betrayed! It

would have been better for that man if he had not been born.". . . [42b]"See, my betrayer is at hand." [43]Immediately, while he was still speaking, Judas came, one of the Twelve, and with him a crowd with swords and clubs, from the chief priests and the scribes and the elders. [44]Now the betrayer had given them a sign, saying, "The one I shall kiss is the man; seize him and lead him away safely." [45]And when he came, he went up to him at once, and said, "Master!" And he kissed him.

Comment: Literally the text identifies Judas as the one disciple of the twelve who betrays Jesus. The Markans, however, understood the kernel of the story (verses 18-21) as a prophecy that all the disciples would betray one of the Twelve sobriety principles, presumably one that spoke of drinking no more. Fulfillment occurs immediately, when the disciples fail to recognize Passover wine as the "desolating abomination" (13.14) and drink the proffered cup (14.23), thereby betraying their recovery program and setting the stage for the emergence of a religion organized around liturgical drinking. This is not to imply that the disciples acted wrongly, only that their destiny was to betray what was probably the first precept of the Twelve by drinking again.

Stricken Shepherd (14.26b-28)

[26b]And they went out to the Mount of Olives. [27]And Jesus said to them, "You will all fall away; for it is written, 'I will strike the shepherd, and the sheep will be scattered.' [28]But after I am raised up, I will go before you to Galilee."

Comment: In this allegory Jesus quotes from Zechariah's Song of the Sword (Zec 13.7-9), which tells of a clerical figure whose demise causes two-thirds of his impenitent flock to perish while one-third choose the refining fire of repentance. Apparently Mark understood the Zecharian prophecy to refer far into the future of the emergent church, specifically to the dissolution of its clergy at its end time. Seemingly he also believed that this event would coincide with the reappearance of the Markôs program, which is the referent of Jesus' remark about resurrection and Galilee.

Denial (14.29-31, 66-72)

[29]Peter said to him, "Even though they all fall away, I will not." [30]And Jesus said to him, "Truly, I say to you, this very night, before the cock crows twice, you will deny me three times." [31]But he said vehemently, "If I must die with you, I will not deny you." And they all said the same. . . . [66]And as Peter was below in the courtyard, one of the maids of the high priest came; [67]and seeing Peter warming himself, she looked at him, and said, "You also were with the Nazarene, Jesus." [68]But he denied it, saying, "I neither know nor understand what you mean." And he went out into the gateway. [69]And the maid saw him, and began again to say to the bystanders, "This man is one of them." [70]But again he denied it. And after a little while again the bystanders said to Peter, "Certainly you are one of them; for you are a Galilean." [71]But he began to invoke a curse on himself and to swear, "I do not know this man of whom you speak." [72]And immediately the cock crowed a second time. And Peter remembered how Jesus had said to him, "Before the cock crows twice, you will deny me three times." And he broke down and wept.

Comment: This story allegorically predicts what actually occurred between Jesus' day and Mark's writing, namely, that many of Jesus' original followers, Christian proto-clergy from Peter on, collectively deny Jesus' alcoholism as well as their own addiction to ritual wine. The identity of the young woman as a female and servant suggests her connection with powerlessness and recovery. Her accusation "you also were with the Nazarene, Jesus," actually means, "You're an alcoholic too!" But Peter denies it vehemently.

Barabbas or Barnasha (15.1-15a)

15 [1]And as soon as it was morning the chief priests, with the elders and scribes, and the whole council held a consultation; and they bound Jesus and led him away and delivered him to Pilate. [2]And Pilate asked him, "Are you the King of the Jews?" And he answered him, "You have said so." [3]And the chief priests accused him of many things. [4]And Pilate again asked him, "Have you no answer to make? See how many charges they bring against you." [5]But Jesus made no further answer, so that Pilate wondered. [6]Now at the feast he used to release for them any one prisoner whom they asked. [7]And among the rebels in prison, who had committed murder in the insurrection, there was a man called Barabbas. [8]And the crowd came up and began to ask Pilate to do as he was wont to do for them.[9]And he answered them, "Do you want me to release for you the King of the Jews?" [10]For he perceived that it was out of envy that the chief priests had delivered him up. [11]But the chief priests stirred up the crowd to have him release for them Barabbas instead. [12]And Pilate again said to them, "Then what shall I do with the man whom you call the King of the Jews?" [13]And they cried out again, "Crucify him." [14]And Pilate said to them, "Why, what evil has he done?" But they shouted all the more, "Crucify him." [15]So Pilate, wishing to satisfy the crowd, released for them Barabbas.

Comment: Here Mark offers his readers the same choice of crucifixion victim that Pilate offers the crowd, the choice between Barabbas and Barnasha (Jesus), that is, between a figure of self-willed militancy and another of humbled anonymity. The allegory was inspired by the Christians' confusion of Jesus and the crucified insurrectionist. "Barabbas," the Aramaic nickname of an otherwise unidentified murderer, meant Son of God in a self-appointed, inflamatory sense. "Barnasha," *ton huion tou anthrōpou* in Greek and son of man in English, was, as repeatedly pointed out, the Aramaic designation Jesus used, sometimes for himself alone and sometimes for himself along with members of the Markôs community. The semantic contrast of these names argues their status as allegorical. So too does the reading in certain manuscripts of Matthew 27.17, "Jesus who is called Barabbas," which suggests that both names belonged to Jesus. If so, Pilate's question would have been, "Which Jesus shall I execute?" This otherwise senseless utterance invites the conclusion that Mark has personified the types represented by the two nicknames, having recognized them as names for the individual before and after surrender. Barabbas is the drunken self-willed zealot who plays God and seeks atonement in violent physical death, whereas Barnasha is the anonymous sober one who has found atonement in dying to self. In his career in Jerusalem, Jesus exemplifies both types, just as all addicts, indeed, all human beings, carry within themselves the persons of Barabbas and Barnasha. Pilate's question thus applies to readers of the gospel in every age, who must decide not only which death to ascribe to the person they assume Jesus to have been but also which death they ultimately choose for themselves, physical death or *psuchē* death, and which of their persons to sacrifice, Barabbas or Barnasha.

Crucifixion (15.15b-39)

[15b]And having scourged Jesus, Pilate delivered him to be crucified. [16]And the soldiers led him away inside the palace; and they called together the whole battalion. [17]And they cloaked him in a purple cloth, and plaiting a crown of thorns they put it on him. [18]And they began to salute him, "Hail, King of the Jews!" [19]And they struck his head with a reed, and spat upon him, and they knelt down in homage to him. [20]And when they had mocked him, they stripped him of his purple cloak, and put his own clothes on him. And they led him out to crucify him. [21]And they compelled a passerby, Simon of Cyrene, who was coming in from the country, the father of Alexander and Rufus, to carry his cross. [22]And they brought him to the place called Golgotha, the skull place. [23]And they offered him wine mingled with myrrh; but he did not take it. [24]And they crucified him, and divided his garments among them, casting lots for them, to decide what each should take. [25]And it was the third hour, when they crucified him. [26]And the inscription of the charge against him read, "The King of the Jews." [27]And with him they crucified two robbers, one on his right and one on his left. [29]And those who passed by derided him, wagging their heads, and saying, "Aha! You would destroy the Temple and build it in three days, [30]save yourself, and come down

from the cross!" [31]So also the chief priests mocked him to one another with the scribes, saying, "He saved others, he cannot save himself. [32]Let the Christ, the King of Israel, come down now from the cross, that we may see and believe." Those who were crucified with him also reviled him. [33]And when the sixth hour had come, there was darkness over the whole land until the ninth hour. [34]And at the ninth hour Jesus cried with a loud voice, *"Eloi, Eloi, lama sabachthani*?" which means, "My God, my God, why hast thou forsaken me?" [35]And some of the bystanders hearing it said, "Behold, he is calling Elijah." [36]And one ran and, filling a sponge full of sour wine, put it on a reed and gave it to him to drink, saying, "Wait, let us see whether Elijah will come to take him down." [37]And Jesus uttered a loud cry, and breathed his last. [38]And the curtain of the Temple was torn in two, from top to bottom. [39]And when the centurion, who stood facing him, saw that he thus breathed his last, he said, "Truly, this man was a son of God."

Comment: Mark's crucifixion narrative is a collage of traditional details culminating in three fictional items of special significance to Markôs readers - the second offer of wine coupled with the Elijah reference, Jesus' refusal via his cry from the cross, and the tearing of the Temple veil (verses 35-38). Only summarized here, the argument surrounding these items is fully laid out in *Mark As Recovery Story*.[15]

In presenting the crucifixion story in the original draft of his book, only a fragment of which survives in a form called Secret Mark, Mark alluded so obviously to Jesus' reputation as an addict that he scandalized Christian readers and was forced to edit his draft for subsequent copying. The result is that readers of Mark have never grasped what the original said. Following is a reconstruction of verses 34-38 as first drafted, with narrator's interjections and restored ellipses in italics:

> [34]And at the ninth hour Jesus cried out in a loud voice, "Eloi, Eloi, lama sabachthani?" [*the Aramaic of Psalm 22.1, "My God, my God, why have you forsaken me?"*]. [35]And some bystanders hearing it [*Eloi, transliterated Aramaic*] *mocked him*, saying, "Behold, he is calling Elijah" [*Elias in Greek*]. [36]And one *of these hecklers* ran and filling a sponge full of sour wine, *tauntingly* put

> it on a reed and offered it to him to drink, saying *sarcastically*, "Wait, let us see whether 'Mr. Elijah' [*referring not to the prophet of old but to Jesus and his reputed Elijah-like abstinence*] will turn and resist it" [*Greek kathaireō, "put down" the temptation to drink the proffered wine*]. [37]But Jesus answered with a loud cry, "O God, I am powerless," and breathed his last. [38]And the curtain in the Temple was torn in two, from top to bottom [*signifying the opening of the presence of God to all who profess powerlessness unto death*].

Everything after the recitation of Ps 22.1, a piece of traditional lore, is a Markan invention intended to reassure Markôs people that, had he been executed, Jesus would have refused drink to the end. As for the Elijah reference, the Markans considered Elijah a fellow water drinker and understood the undrunk Elijah cup at Passover to mean that Elijah comes but drinks no wine. They considered it a veiled sign of Messiah, of an age of sobriety wherein the joy of wine is found not in drinking it but in choosing to leave it undrunk. As for Jesus, insofar as he was known at all outside the Cupmaster fellowship prior to his disappearance, he was known as a former wine addict. It was not surprising, therefore, that Mark would employ Jesus' reputation and the Markans' image of Elijah as raw material in his account of a heckler offering Jesus wine.

The most important element of the story is the reconstructed cry from the cross, "O God, I am powerless." While Mark mentions the cry, its content is conspicuously absent from his text as we know it. The cry represented here is a reconstruction of Mark's original version, literally, "My power, O Power, has entirely left me," by way of verse 19 of the Gospel of Peter. Apparently the writer of the Gospel of Peter found the cry in Secret Mark just as worded here, but then, supposing it a garbled version of Ps 22.1, changed it from third to second person and introduced the awkward double vocative that appears in the Gospel of Peter, "My Power, O Power, you have entirely left me." Mark omitted Jesus' cry of powerlessness from subsequent copies of his book, probably because it was rejected by suspicious Christian readers. Nor could he even hint at the connection between the cry and the notice about the tearing of the Temple veil, whose inclusion at this point has always proved a puzzle to interpreters. The narrator's explanation in verse 38 as reconstructed makes the connection explicit.

Mark ends his crucifixion narrative with the centurion's profession (verse 39), a fiction intended to placate both Roman censors and gentile Christian hierarchs, two groups whose approval was necessary if his book was to gain acceptance and survive. Mark expected the Romans to interpret the centurion's "Son of God" in its secular sense as designating a divine figure superior to ordinary mortals and an exemplar of the civil order that the Romans would demand in the postwar period. On the other hand, Mark hoped that Son of God understood in its religious sense, as a synonym for Messiah, would distract Christian readers from the preceding events in the cross narrative. As ritual drinkers, Christian clergymen might be scandalized by the memory of Jesus as an addict whose last words were a refusal of drink, but their anger should change to delight at the evangelical implications of a Roman pagan professing him Messiah.

Rock Tomb (15.42-46)

42And when evening had come, since it was the day of preparation, that is, the day before the sabbath, 43Joseph of Arimathea, a respected member of the council, who was also himself looking for the Rule of God, took courage and went to Pilate, and asked for the body of Jesus. 44And Pilate wondered if he were already dead; and summoning the centurion, he asked him whether he was already dead. 45And when he learned from the centurion that he was dead, he granted the body to Joseph. 46And he bought a linen shroud, and taking him down, wrapped him in the linen shroud, and laid him in a tomb which had been hewed out of the rock; and he rolled a stone against the door of the tomb.

Comment: The rock tomb represents the encrypting of the story of Jesus' alcoholism by the church of Peter, whose name in Greek means rock. Despite his Pentecost proclamation of Jesus' sobriety program (Acts 2.14-36[16]), Peter's subsequent quarter-century witness to a nonalcoholic Jesus provided Christians a foundation upon which to build an ecclesiastical structure wherein the memory of a powerless and surrendered Jesus would be anathema, to be hidden away and forgotten.

The note linking Joseph of Arimathea to the Rule of God may reflect a memory that a sanhedrin member by that name, having initially reached out to the Cupmasters in search of sobriety (the Rule of God), had thereafter, whether from ignorance or guile, authored the report of Jesus' death.

Women (15.40-41, 47; 16.1-4, 7-8)

[15.40]There were also women looking on from afar, among whom were Mary Magdalene, and Mary the mother of James the younger and of Joses, and Salome, [41]who, when he was in Galilee, followed him, and ministered to him; and also many other women who came up with him to Jerusalem. . . . [47]Mary Magdalene and Mary the mother of Joses saw where he was laid.

16 [1]And when the sabbath was past, Mary Magdalene, Mary the mother of James, and Salome brought spices, so that they might go and anoint him. [2]And very early on the first day of the week they went to the tomb when the sun had risen. [3]And they were saying to one another, "Who will roll away the stone for us from the door of the tomb?" [4]And looking up, they saw that the stone was rolled back; for it was very large. . . . [7]*And the young man said to them,* "Go, tell his disciples and Peter that he is going before you in Galilee; there you will see him, as he told you." [8]And they went out and fled from the tomb; for trembling and astonishment had come upon them; and they said nothing to any one, for they were afraid.

Comment: The women watching from afar (15.40-41) represent Markôs people observing the process through which, in the months and years following his disappearance, the Jesus whose story they knew firsthand was transformed to crucifixion victim, resurrected Messiah, and church founder. Their fearful refusal to tell Peter and the other disciples the news that Jesus has escaped the tomb and returned to Galilee (16.7-8), always a puzzle to interpreters, represents a cautionary prophecy of the future reappearance of the Markôs program and emancipation of Jesus' story, and of how frightening it will be to sober people at that time to speak of Jesus' alcoholism to church people, how difficult to proclaim his recovery story, and how easy to say nothing to anyone.

Young Man in White (14.51-52; 16.5-7)

14.51 And a young man followed him, with nothing but a linen cloth about his body; and they seized him, 52 but he left the linen cloth and ran away naked. . . .

16.5 And entering the tomb, the women saw a young man sitting on the right side, wearing a white stole; and they were amazed. 6 And he said to them, "Do not be amazed; you seek Jesus of Nazareth, who was crucified. He has risen, he is not here; see the place where they laid him. 7 But go, tell his disciples and Peter that he is going before you in Galilee; there you will see him, as he told you."

Comment: The young man in 14.51-52 is Mark himself, depicted in a bit of autobiography injected into the narrative of Jesus' arrest. Apparently it was on Passover night that John Mark first entered the fellowship from which he derived his surname. A fuller account of Mark's meeting with Jesus is contained in Secret Mark:

> And Jesus . . . stretched forth his hand and raised the youth, seizing his hand. And the youth, looking upon him, loved him and began to beseech him that he might be with him. And going out of the tomb they came into the house of the youth, for he was rich. And . . . Jesus told him what to do and in the evening the youth comes to him, wearing a linen cloth over his naked body. And he remained with him that night, for Jesus taught him the mystery of the Rule of God.[17]

The resurrection shown here symbolizes recovery from the living death of addiction. The youth's "loving him" and "beseeching him to be with him" are evidence not of homoeroticism, as some have claimed, but of the young man's desire for sobriety, of wanting to be with sober people and to have what sober people have, emotions characteristic of newcomers to recovery. The linen cloth and naked body symbolize the youth's completion of a process similar to the inventory and admission of wrongs practiced in Twelve-Step programs today, a process involving divestiture of all signs of wealth and station and a stripping of pride and ego as prerequisite to membership in the egalitarian Cupmaster fellowship. The "mystery of the Rule of God" refers to the Twelve sobriety precepts and other recovery lore. Thus began Mark's affiliation with the Rule of God, which continued through the writing of his gospel nearly forty years later.

If the young man in 14.51-52 represents Mark the initiate into the Rule of God, the figure in the tomb (16.5-7) is Mark the annunciator of a restored Markôs program at the endtime of the Christian church. His linen garment (*sindōn*, 14.51) has become a stole (*stōle*, 16.5), the sign of evangelistic office. As Mark's prophetic alter ego, the man exhorts the women (recovering alcoholics in the future era) to stop looking for the risen (sober and spiritually awakened) Jesus in the rock tomb of Jerusalem (the church of Peter, emblem of stage-one sobriety), but instead to tell Peter and the disciples (religious drinkers in the endtime) to seek him in Galilee (symbolic locus of stage-two sobriety in the revived Cupmaster fellowship).

Very Early on the Third Day (16.4)

[4]And very early on the first day of the week they went to the tomb when the sun had risen.

Comment: The women visit the tomb "very early on the first day of the week," that is, on the morning of the third day of entombment. Aware of the ancient Christian belief placing the resurrection "on the third day" (I Corinthians 15.4), Mark situates the discovery of the empty tomb at the very beginning of that day. Allegorically, Jesus' release and return to Galilee represent a future revival of the Markôs movement, and "very early" on the third day locates that event at the beginning of a third era or age.

Apparently Mark and his confreres believed the Cupmaster fellowship likely to die out in post-war Judea, proscribed by the angry Romans as just another Jewish sect and anathematized by Jewish Christians on account of its counter-Christian memory of Jesus. Yet they also believed that Jesus' words at the Last Supper, "poured out for the recovery of many" (14.24), promised a time of universal sobriety after a lengthy period of worsening addiction among humankind, the time of the reappearance of their fellowship.

When did they think this would occur? The answer may lie in the Book of Revelation. Interpreting the core of that book as the work of an end-of-century Markan who apocalyptically prophesies Christendom's recovery from addiction, *Mark As Recovery Story* suggests that, in the section of Revelation dealing with the universal final judgment, the six mentions of a period of "one thousand years" (Rev 20.2-7) are a garbled version of the writer's original text containing *three* mentions of a *two*-thousand-year period expressed in the conventional Semitic way, "after a thousand years and another thousand years."[18] If so, it means that the Markans believed, for whatever reasons, that their Messianic program with its Twelve sobriety precepts would reappear at the dawning of a third millennium. From today's perspective, that time would be now and the manifestation of this second coming would be the Twelve Steps and the spiritual fellowship of Alcoholics Anonymous.

Thus ends Sobriety Mark, a gospel that begins by announcing the sobriety story of one person and concludes by prophesying the future recovery of all humanity in a sunlit age of serenity and harmony under the Rule of God.

Notes

1. *Mark as Recovery Story*, 27-30, gives the linguistic argument for this translation, based upon the grammatical structure of the phrase (modifier plus nominal) in the Septuagint.

2. *Recovery Story*, 52-55.

3. Dwight N. Peterson ("A Gimp's-eye View of the Healing of the Paralytic in Mark 2.1-12," paper presented to the 1996 Annual Meeting of the Society of Biblical Literature, New Orleans) finds these meanings attested in Athenaeus, *Deipnosophiste*, 2.2.31.

4. *Recovery Story* documents the ambiguity and multiple referentiality of "son of man" as studied by Matthew Black, Geza Vermes, Barnabas Lindars, and P. Maurice Casey.

5. *Recovery Story*, 195-196.

6. *Recovery Story*, 295n13. Casey defines what he calls the general use of the term as instances when a speaker wishes to say something about himself and a group of associates.

7. *Recovery Story*, chap. 3, "Isaiah's Servant Drunkard," 87-115.

8. This translation, a composite based on the work of Mitchell Dahood, G.R. Driver, and D.J.A. Clines, is discussed in *Recovery Story*, 98, 102, and 107-108.

9. *Recovery Story*, 211-212. Geza Vermes finds this anecdote in the Babylonian Talmud, Erubin 53b. George Lamsa discusses the northern Aramaic homonymity of donkey and wine in *More Light on the Gospel* (Garden City, N.Y.: Doubleday, 1968), 47-48 and 74.

10. Mitchell Dahood, *The Anchor Bible Psalms I* (Garden City, N.Y.: Doubleday, 1965), 86-91, emended. *Recovery Story* discusses the basis of the emendation, 180-181.

11. Note 2 above.

12. This version is based on Mitchell Dahood, *The Anchor Bible Psalms III* (Garden City, N.Y.: Doubleday, 1970), 144-151.

13. See "Introduction," note 7.

14. C.H. Turner, "Markan Usage: Notes, Critical and Exegetical, on the Second Gospel, VIII," *Journal of Theological Studies* 28 (1926-27): 249-262.

15. *Recovery Story*, 74-81.

16. *Recovery Story*, 161-165 and 168-183. Peter's finest hour occurs at Pentecost, beginning with his denial of the charges of drunkenness leveled at the apostles, then including his proclamation of Jesus' recovery program to the multitude and his sermon interpreting Joel and Psalm 16 as prophecies of that program (Acts 2.14-36).

17. Smith, *Clement of Alexandria*, 447.

18. *Recovery Story*, 261-262. The core content of Revelation (10.1-19.21) is interpreted as the work of an end-of-century former addict in a remnant Markôs group, who identifies alcoholism as the besetting illness of the fledgling churches, then prophecies their future recovery.

Afterword

Historicity Is the dual-audience theory of Mark sufficiently well supported to warrant a conclusion of historical actuality? My answer is yes. The evidence is far too substantial to be discounted. Not only are the ambiguities too numerous and the ellipses too pointed to be incidental, their consistent alignment along the Christian/sobriety axis cannot be the result of coincidence. Nor can it be accidental that the sobriety perspective explains nearly every textual feature that Christian scholarship has considered problematic. In short, I do not think one can reasonably view these items as the product of chance rather than of the author's intention. And if they are intentional, then the two audiences were actual—unless one chooses to believe that Mark, writing in a time of crisis and extreme peril, was merely a trickster bent on hoaxing the Christians. Nor are these textual features the result of Mark's being the awkward writer he is often accused of being; rather they identify him as having crafted one of history's most ingenious works of literary camouflage.

Jesus as Addict So I think we can say with historical certainty that Mark wrote for two principal audiences in 68 A.D., one of which consisted of former inebriates. But does that mean that Jesus himself was an ex-addict? I believe it does. Mk 14.51-52 suggests that a youthful Mark met Jesus in person, and Secret Mark shows Jesus receiving him into the Rule of God. Clearly, Mark knew whether or not Jesus was alcoholic. If Jesus' addiction lacked a basis in fact, then all the ambiguities and sobriety emblems in the gospel, the discourse on wine and the Gethsemane surrender and so on, are nothing more than fictions aimed at creating a persona with which addicts could identify. Christians would not have recognized much less valorized such a persona and would have regarded any document containing it as worthless. But the Christians *did* accept Mark's book, including enigmas such as the water carrier (14.13) and scandalous items such as "he is *existēmi*" (3.21). The point is, Mark would not have risked writing what he did if he had not known that the addict persona was factual and that behind their denial and selective recall the

Jewish-Christian elders of the day also knew that it was factual. Nor did he act a moment too soon. Repression was taking its toll on Christian memory, and Matthew was able, in adapting Mark shortly after the Roman War, to omit both of the troubling items just cited along with a surprisingly large number of the Markan ambiguities without fear of reproach from his co-religionists.

Crucifixion As for crucifixion, we must bear in mind that we are speaking about a person whom the Jewish officials knew only as a drunken and vituperative Passover pilgrim who had acted out in the Temple court. The Jesus of Sobriety Mark was not a religious reformer or insurrectionist, he was an intoxicated man who caused a commotion by haranguing fellow pilgrims and grabbing madly at their drinking vessels. The Temple police probably quelled the disturbance he caused almost as soon as it began. There is no evidence that the Romans even noticed it. Nor did Jesus ever unambiguously claim to be Messiah or Son of God, an action that could have led to crucifixion. True, his reputation as an "unbridled drunkard" (Mt 11.19/Lk 7.34 based on Dt 21.20) stamped him as the "stubborn and rebellious son" of Dt 21.21, hence subject to execution by stoning. By the time of his arrest, however, Jesus was sober and humbled, his combative messianism forever history. It is absurd to think that enlightened Jewish leaders in the first century would have sought to take such a person's life, much less to do so by procuring a Roman crucifixion. In fact, the Tosephta (Sanhedrin 71) quotes a rabbinic interpretation of Dt 21.18-21 so limited as to make it virtually impossible to invoke a sentence of execution. "There never has been a stubborn and rebellious son," wrote the rabbis, "and never will be." No doubt there was a crucifixion on Passover in 30 A.D., but I am fairly sure that the Markans believed the victim to have been someone other than Jesus.

Then and Now In what ways do the practices of the ancient Cupmaster fellowship resemble those of Alcoholics Anonymous? We can be reasonably sure about the following items: Both movements renounce alcohol in favor of some other drink emblematic of sobriety—water in the case of the Markans, and coffee, stereotypically, in the case of A.A. Both involve meetings consisting of a talk by a speaker followed by comments from all present. Some meetings are closed to nonmembers while others are open to everyone. Members of both movements speak of God as a Power greater than self. Both developed twelve sobriety precepts, the Markôs Twelve and the Twelve Steps. The first three of the Twelve may have been:

> We declared we would drink no more of the fruit of the vine (14.25).
>
> Admitted that God has all power (14.36a).
>
> Humbly asked him to remove our cup addiction (14.36b).

Both movements believe that further drinking is the best advice for persons still lacking a desire to stop; and both find that sobriety comes in two stages, victory over drink followed by victory over self. Although Jesus in the grip of messianism argued with Jewish religious officials, Cupmasters and A.A.s, once sober, keep recovery and religion separate. They disavow authority over others, try to tell the whole truth about themselves, practice gratitude, and give the credit to God. Both put the importance of sobriety ahead of familial ties, wealth, or social station. Markôs people and A.A.s both attest to a changing of mind and spiritual awakening. Both practice anonymity and place principles before personalities. And both consider the capstone of recovery to be spiritual awakening and service carrying the message to others. Indeed, the last precept of the Twelve may have resembled A.A.'s twelfth step, perhaps as follows:

> Having suffered much (9.12) and so been glorified (13.26), we proclaimed the Rule of God to drinkers and gave ourselves in service for the recovery of many (10.45).

Final Thoughts Summing up, I think we can be quite certain that the Gospel of Mark was intended for two groups of readers living in Palestine at the time of its writing, Jewish Christians and Markôs insiders. We can be reasonably confident that the recovering wine addict depicted in Sobriety Mark is a portrait of Jesus as Mark and his cohort remembered him, perhaps from hearing him tell his sobriety story in Galilee in the years following 30 A.D. Certainly we can see that the spirituality of the Cupmasters resembled in key particulars that of Alcoholics Anonymous today. And there are good reasons for concluding that Jesus' path to atonement led not to a cross on Golgotha but to the humbling ground of Gethsemane.

I hope that members of the scholarly community will, upon reflection, be able to get beyond their understandable skepticism about these matters and see that the Greek Gospel of Mark is a text whose interpretation is by no means settled, that problems in its translation remain whose solutions require far more than merely "playing with prepositions," and that its grammatical and lexical richness deserves deeper linguistic analysis and more creative modes of representation in languages of translation, than it has hitherto received from scholars blindered by the Christian mindset. I myself am convinced that the key to the historical Jesus is not in Galilean archaeology, non-canonical gospels, or Jesus seminars, however interesting these may be, but in the Greek text of John the Markôs.

On a different note, I hope that my friends in Twelve-Step programs have found in Sobriety Mark a Jesus with whom they can share the profound experience of addiction and recovery—not in the unreal way in which Jesus is said to have been like us in all things but sin, but in the same authentic way in which we former addicts share our experiences of suffering and happy destiny with those of Bill W. and Dr. Bob (William Griffith Wilson, 1895-1971, and Robert Holbrook Smith, 1879-1950), founders of the Twelve-Step movement in our day just as Jesus was in his.

Bibliographical Note

My chief sources of textual and linguistic information on New Testament Greek are the following:

Greek texts. I have used the Greek text of Mark from Alfred Marshall's *The R.S.V. Interlinear Greek-English New Testament* (Grand Rapids: Zondervan, 1981). This work contains the Revised Standard Version, copyrighted 1946 by the Division of Christian Education of the National Council of Churches of Christ in the United States of America, which I have quoted in full. For manuscript variants I have used Reuben Swanson's *New Testament Greek Manuscripts—Mark* (Sheffield, England: Sheffield Academic Press, 1995). For a consensus of scholarly opinion on the historicity of Jesus' sayings I have consulted Robert Funk's *The Gospel of Mark—Red Letter Edition* (Sonoma, CA: Polebridge Press, 1991).

Greek lexicons. I have relied most upon W.E. Vine's *Expository Dictionary of New Testament Words* (Grand Rapids: Zondervan, 1952), and Harold K. Moulton's *The Analytical Greek Lexicon Revised* (Grand Rapids: Zondervan, 1978), along with Robert G. Bratcher and Eugene A. Nida's *A Translator's Handbook on the Gospel of Mark* (Leiden, The Netherlands: E.J. Brill, 1961). I have also used H.G. Liddell and R. Scott's *A Greek-English Lexicon* (Oxford: Clarendon Press, 1925); W. Bauer, W.F. Arndt, and F.W. Gingrich's *A Greek-English Lexicon of the New Testament*, 2d ed. (Chicago: University of Chicago Press, 1979); and G.W.H. Lampe's *A Patristic Greek Lexicon* (Oxford: Clarendon Press, 1961).

Greek grammar. Max Zerwick and Mary Grosvenor, *A Grammatical Analysis of the Greek New Testament* (Rome: Biblical Institute Press, 1981).

The translations comprised by Sobriety Mark are largely unprecedented in Markan scholarship, although prior studies (cited in *Mark as Recovery Story*) frequently served as springboards to the insights reflected here. To illustrate, consider the two Markan nicknames: I discovered in Seán P. Kealy's *Mark's*

Gospel: A History of Its Interpretation (New York: Paulist Press, 1982, 51) that a Hebrew etymology of Mark (*mar kôs*, "master of the cup") is mentioned by the seventeenth-century exegete Cornelius à Lapide. At that point it occurred to me to construe the name as a coterie designation for former wine addict. Much later I was surprised to find that the unnamed writer of the Anti-Marcionite Prologue, which I ran across in Vincent Taylor's *The Gospel according to St. Mark* (London: Macmillan, 1952, 30), speaks of "Mark who is called 'stump-fingered' [*colobodactylus*] because he had rather small fingers in comparison with the rest of his body." Taylor points to the likely authenticity of the name owing to its oddity, but suggests that it may have had a meaning less obvious than that ascribed to it by the writer of the Prologue. When the meaning "unable to grasp a drinking cup" occurred to me, I realized that the semantic intersection of the two names, Markôs and stump-fingered, identifies them as twin witnesses to sobriety.

For another example, virtually all scholarly commentaries on the gospel note the oddity and inappropriateness of various aspects of Mark's word usage, for instance, two verbs in the baptism pericope (1.9-13). One is *schizō*, denoting a rending or splitting assunder, which describes Jesus' vision of the heavens opening; here one would expect a less violent and more portentous verb such as *anaptussō*. The other is *ekballō*, a forceful throwing or casting out often used in the exorcism of demons, which describes the action of the Spirit impelling Jesus to go into the wilderness; here one might expect a milder term such as *anagō*, the word that Matthew (4.1) in fact substitutes for the Markan original. Alerted to many items like these, I found in almost every case that the perspective of Sobriety Mark provides a coherent explanation of lexical choices that have heretofore baffled commentators, who all too often have reacted by accusing the gospel writer, a master of literary camouflage, of linguistic ineptitude.

Also, I found that an alternative reading proposed in the research may have implications that the researcher has ignored or failed to pursue. I noted, for instance, that several versions of Mark render *auto pinō kainon* (14.25) as "I drink new wine," but that none remarks the dual referentiality of "fruit of the vine" and *auto pinō kainon* that results when "I drink new wine" is chosen instead of the pronominalized form, "I drink it new."

And of course, where no one has suggested a particular line of interpretation, there is nothing to document. To the best of my knowledge, for example, no one has ever applied the Northern Aramaic "donkey/wine" pun in interpreting the stage business preceding the Jerusalem entrance (11.2-7); no one has ever seen the apocalyptic "desolating sacrilege" (13.14) as liturgical drink or the undrunk Elijah cup as a sign of sobriety; no one has explored the implications of the fact that *poieō* in 3.14 can mean formulated as well as appointed; and no one has recognized that *parerchomai* in 14.35 (and 6.48) can mean to get through a situation as well as to avoid it.

Finally, many important insights came to me wholly apart from academia, from my experiences in sobriety. For example, the first recovery story I heard was told by a Catholic priest who had nearly died from esophageal bleeding caused by drink. Home from hospital, weak and shaken, he told how he sat on his bed drinking when suddenly, in a moment of insight, he recognized drink as the cause of his bloodshed. He hurled the bottle against the wall and never drank again. His story stayed with me, but years passed before I realized that the priest's words over his bottle echoed the meaning of Jesus' words over the Passover cup, "This is my blood" (14.24). Some further examples: how my first sponsor's sudden death taught me that it is principles, not persons, that are Messiah; how a fall from an apple tree while playing prophet at a Trappist monastery gave me my first lesson about ego death and stage-two recovery; how pondering Mark 13.14 one beautiful summer afternoon changed forever the way I view the wine chalice in the Christian Eucharistic service. It should not have been surprising, I suppose, that spiritual truths would arise more readily from autobiography than bibliography.